Area C and the Future
of the Palestinian Economy

A WORLD BANK STUDY

Area C and the Future of the Palestinian Economy

Orhan Niksic, Nur Nasser Eddin, and Massimiliano Cali

THE WORLD BANK
Washington, D.C.

© 2014 International Bank for Reconstruction and Development / The World Bank
1818 H Street NW, Washington, DC 20433
Telephone: 202-473-1000; Internet: www.worldbank.org

Some rights reserved

1 2 3 4   17 16 15 14

World Bank Studies are published to communicate the results of the Bank's work to the development community with the least possible delay. The manuscript of this paper therefore has not been prepared in accordance with the procedures appropriate to formally edited texts.

This work is a product of the staff of The World Bank with external contributions. The findings, interpretations, and conclusions expressed in this work do not necessarily reflect the views of The World Bank, its Board of Executive Directors, or the governments they represent. The World Bank does not guarantee the accuracy of the data included in this work. The boundaries, colors, denominations, and other information shown on any map in this work do not imply any judgment on the part of The World Bank concerning the legal status of any territory or the endorsement or acceptance of such boundaries.

Nothing herein shall constitute or be considered to be a limitation upon or waiver of the privileges and immunities of The World Bank, all of which are specifically reserved.

Rights and Permissions

This work is available under the Creative Commons Attribution 3.0 IGO license (CC BY 3.0 IGO) http://creativecommons.org/licenses/by/3.0/igo. Under the Creative Commons Attribution license, you are free to copy, distribute, transmit, and adapt this work, including for commercial purposes, under the following conditions:

Attribution—Please cite the work as follows: Niksic, Orhan, Nur Nasser Eddin, and Massimiliano Cali. 2014. *Area C and the Future of the Palestinian Economy*. World Bank Studies. Washington, DC: World Bank. doi:10.1596/978-1-4648-0193-8. License: Creative Commons Attribution CC BY 3.0 IGO

Translations—If you create a translation of this work, please add the following disclaimer along with the attribution: *This translation was not created by The World Bank and should not be considered an official World Bank translation. The World Bank shall not be liable for any content or error in this translation.*

Adaptations—If you create an adaptation of this work, please add the following disclaimer along with the attribution: *This is an adaptation of an original work by The World Bank. Responsibility for the views and opinions expressed in the adaptation rests solely with the author or authors of the adaptation and are not endorsed by The World Bank.*

Third-party content—The World Bank does not necessarily own each component of the content contained within the work. The World Bank therefore does not warrant that the use of any third-party-owned individual component or part contained in the work will not infringe on the rights of those third parties. The risk of claims resulting from such infringement rests solely with you. If you wish to re-use a component of the work, it is your responsibility to determine whether permission is needed for that re-use and to obtain permission from the copyright owner. Examples of components can include, but are not limited to, tables, figures, or images.

All queries on rights and licenses should be addressed to the Publishing and Knowledge Division, The World Bank, 1818 H Street NW, Washington, DC 20433, USA; fax: 202-522-2625; e-mail: pubrights@worldbank.org.

ISBN (paper): 978-1-4648-0193-8
ISBN (electronic): 978-1-4648-0196-9
DOI: 10.1596/978-1-4648-0193-8

Cover photo: © World Bank.
Cover design: Debra Naylor, Naylor Designs.

Contents

Acknowledgments		*ix*
Abbreviations		*xi*
Executive Summary		1
	Direct Benefits	3
	Indirect Benefits	4
Chapter 1	**The Palestinian Economy, Israeli Restrictions, and the Potential of Area C**	9
	The Palestinian Economy: Volatility, Distorted Growth, and Uncertain Prospects	9
	Restrictions on Movement and Access, and the Stunted Potential of Area C	11
Chapter 2	**Area C—Output Potential of Key Sectors of the Palestinian Economy**	17
	Agriculture	17
	Dead Sea Minerals	21
	Stone Mining and Quarrying	23
	Construction and Real Estate	25
	Tourism and the Dead Sea	30
	Telecommunications	36
	Cosmetics	41
Chapter 3	**Indirect Benefits**	47
	Secondary Costs and Benefits Related to Infrastructure	47
	Movement	47
	Water and Wastewater	48
	Telecommunications	48
	Institutional Infrastructure	49
	Secondary Costs and Benefits Related to Spillover Effects	50
	Potential Indirect Benefits	51
	Potential Fiscal Benefits	52

Appendix A	Methodological Notes	55
Appendix B	Agriculture Section Tables	71
Appendix C	Relevant Legal Agreements	75

Bibliography   81

Boxes

1.1	Limited Access to Education for Palestinians Who Live in Area C Increases Their Chance of Being Poor	14
2.1	Agriculture in Israeli Settlements in Area C Exemplifies the Sector's Potential in the Area	20
2.2	Fighting the Current Restrictions to Develop a New City	27
2.3	Serving the Residents of Marah Rabah and Teqou in Area B	37
2.4	Suboptimal Transmission Paths	39

Figures

ES.1	Growth Generated Through the Lifting of Restrictions Could Increase Potential Palestinian Value Added by USD 3.4 Billion	6
ES.2	If the Output Potential Associated with Lifting the Restrictions Materializes, the Fiscal Deficit of the PA Is Reduced by 56 Percent and the Need for External Budget Support Greatly Declines	7
1.1	Real GDP Growth Rate 1999–First Half 2013	10
1.2	The Decline in the Tradable Sectors	11
2.1	Agriculture Value Added in the West Bank	17
2.2	Share of Agriculture in Total Employment, West Bank	18
2.3	West Bank Labor Productivity	19
2.4	Potash Price and Demand Projections, 2012–25	22
2.5	World Production of Bromine	23
2.6	While Stone and Mineral Exports Have Increased in Nominal Terms, Their Share in Total Exports Dropped Despite a Meager Overall Export Growth	24
2.7	Growth in Housing Construction in the West Bank, 1967–2007	28
2.8	Housing Prices and Palestinian CPI, 1996–2012 (1996=100)	30
2.9	Following the Second Intifada, the Employment in the Hotel and Restaurants Sector (A Good Proxy for Tourism) Doubled	31
2.10	Following the Second Intifada, the Number of Hotels Increased Only Modestly, but Hotel Activity Increased Dramatically	31
2.11	Number of International Tourist Arrivals in the Palestinian Territories (1000)	32

3.1	Telecommunications Sector Output Purchased by Other Sectors of the Economy	49
3.2	Palestinian Tourism's Reliance on Inputs from Agriculture and Agroprocessing	50
A.1	The Effects of The Restrictions on Price and Quantity of Construction	61

Tables

1.1	Significance of Area C in Terms of Natural Resources	12
2.1	Palestinian Permits in Rural Areas and in Area C	26
2.2	Estimated Population Growth and Area C Restrictiveness in the West Bank Governorates	28
2.3	Selected Dead Sea Tourism Indicators for Jordan and Israel	34
2.4	The Number of Tourists Has Been Growing Around the World and Is Expected to Continue with Strong Growth by 2020 Worldwide and in the Middle East	35
2.5	Revenues Collected from West Bank Sites Managed and Operated by the Israeli Nature and Parks Authority	36
3.1	Potential Revenue and Deficit Reduction	52
A.1	Calculation of Value Added for Potash Production	59
A.2	Annual Potential Revenues Lost by the Palestinian Mobile Operators Due to the Restrictions	62
A.3	Annual Costs Incurred by the Palestinian Mobile Operators Due to the Inability to Freely Operate in Area C	63
A.4	Annual Potential Revenues Lost by the Palestinian Landline Operator Due to the Area C Restrictions	64
A.5	Annual Costs Incurred by the Palestinian Landline Operator Due to the Area C Restrictions	65
B.1	Value of Production Per Dunum and Cultivated Area, Irrigated vs. Rain-fed, Fruit Trees	71
B.2	Value of Production per Dunum and Cultivated Area, Irrigated vs. Rain-fed, Field Crops	72
B.3	Value of Production Per Dunum and Cultivated Area, Irrigated vs. Rain-fed, Vegetables	73

Acknowledgments

This report was prepared and written by a team of World Bank staff led by Orhan Niksic, Senior Economist (MNSED), and also included Nur Nasser Eddin, Economist (MNSED), and Massimiliano Cali, Economist (PRMTR). Duja Michael, a consultant, assisted the Bank team in conducting research and analysis for the report.

The report benefited considerably from overall guidance and comments provided by Mariam Sherman, the World Bank Country Director for West Bank and Gaza, Manuela Ferro, Director (LCRVP), and Bernard Funck, Sector Manager (MNSED). The following peer reviewers also provided most valuable comments: Dr. Salam Fayyad, former Prime Minister of the Palestinian Authority, Kaspar Richter, Lead Economist (ECA PREM), John Nasir, Economic Adviser (OPSPQ), Tracey Lane, Senior Economist (SASGP). Furthermore, much gratitude for time and efforts to enhance the quality of this report is owed to Shanta Devarajan, Chief Economist (MNACE), Nigel Roberts, (former West Bank and Gaza Country Director), Tara Vishwanath, Lead Economist (MNSED), Nandini Krishnan, Economist (MNSED), and Ranan Ibrahim Al-Muthaffar, Operations Officer (MNCGZ).

Undoubtedly, this report could not have been produced without the data, information, and insights provided by colleagues in the Palestinian Central Bureau of Statistics, Ministry of Tourism and Antiquities of the Palestinian National Authority, Ministry of Planning of the Palestinian National Authority, ARIJ and its director Jad Isaac, Nicola Harrison (UNRWA), Rana Hannoun (FAO), Bader Rock, Private Sector and Trade Adviser (Office of the Quartet Representative), and several prominent representatives of the Palestinian private sector.

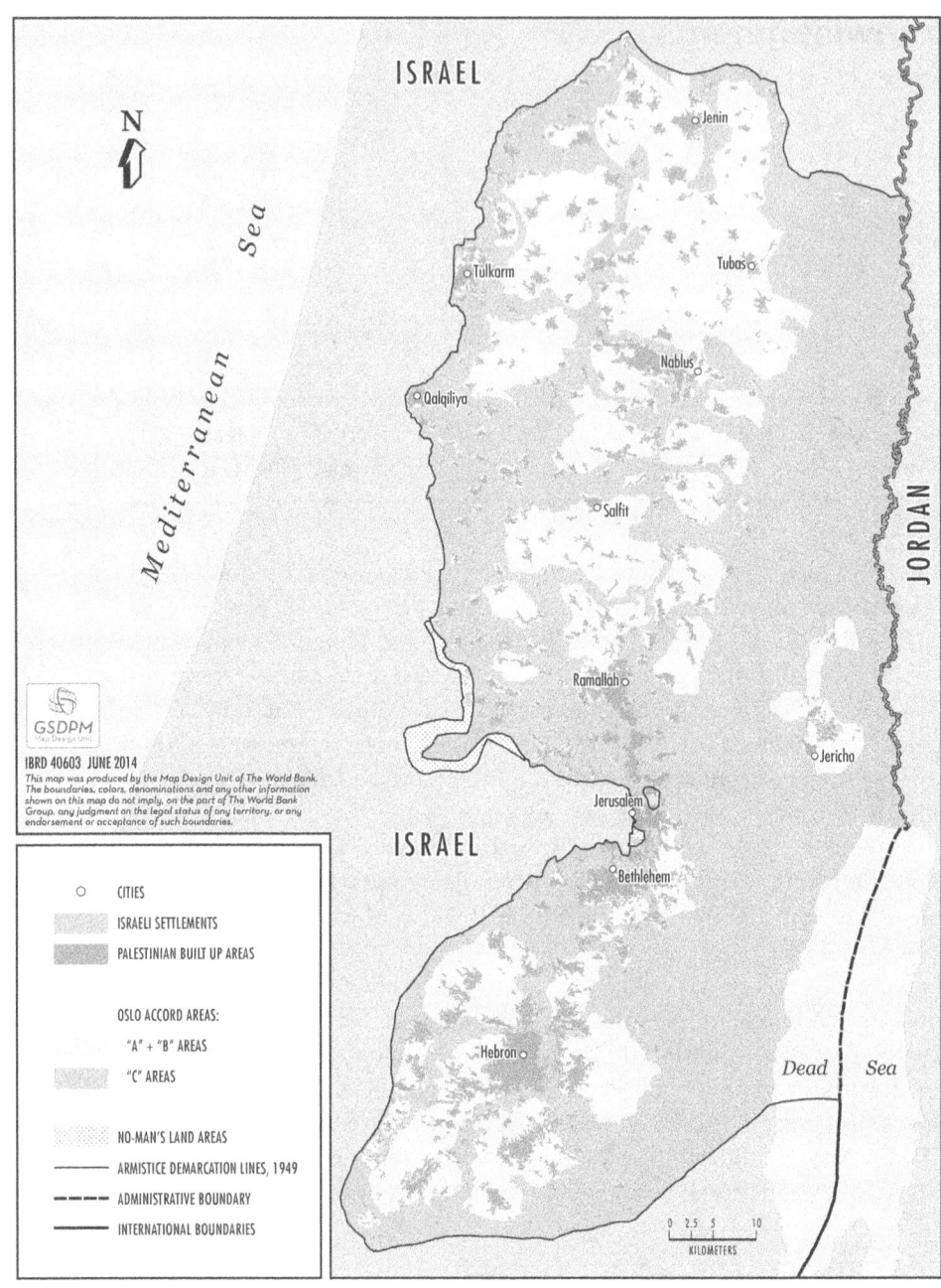

Abbreviations

ADSL	asymmetric digital subscriber line
ARIJ	Applied Research Institute in Jerusalem
CAC	Civil Affairs Coordination and Cooperation Committee
COGAT	Coordinator of Government Activities in the Territories
CPI	consumer price index
DOP	Declaration of Principles
FAO	Food and Agriculture Organization
FDI	foreign direct investment
GDP	gross domestic product
GOI	Government of Israel
ICA	Israeli Civil Administration
ICL	Israeli Chemicals Ltd
IDF	Israeli Defence Forces
IMF	International Monetary Fund
IPCC	International Peace and Cooperation Centre
ISP	Internet Service Providers
IT	information technology
ITU	International Telecommunication Union
JTC	Joint Technical Committee
JWC	Joint Water Committee
LRC	Land Research Center
MCM	million cubic meter
MoF	Ministry of Finance
NBP	National Blueprint
NGO	nongovernmental organization
OCHA	United Nations Office for the Coordination of Humanitarian Affairs
PA	Palestinian Authority
PCBS	Palestinian Central Bureau of Statistics

PLO	Palestinian Liberation Organization
UNESCO	United Nations Educational, Scientific and Cultural Organization
UNIDO	United Nations Industrial Development Organization
UNWTO	United Nations World Tourism Organization
USD	United States Dollars

Executive Summary

Restrictions on economic activity in Area C of the West Bank have been particularly detrimental to the Palestinian economy. Area C constitutes about 61 percent of the West Bank territory. It is defined by the 1995 Israeli-Palestinian Interim Agreement on the West Bank and the Gaza Strip as "areas of the West Bank outside Areas A and B, which, except for the issues that will be negotiated in the permanent status negotiations, will be gradually transferred to Palestinian jurisdiction in accordance with this Agreement."[1] According to the Interim Agreement, the gradual transfer should have been completed by 1997.[2] However, it has not been implemented as envisaged in the Interim Agreement[3] and in the meantime, access to this area for most kinds of economic activity has been severely limited. Yet, the potential contribution of Area C to the Palestinian economy is large. Area C is richly endowed with natural resources and it is contiguous, whereas Areas A and B are smaller territorial islands. The manner in which Area C is currently administered virtually precludes Palestinian businesses from investing there.

Mobilizing the Area C potential would help a faltering Palestinian economy. The Palestinian economy has experienced strong growth in recent years, fuelled by large inflows of donor budget support, some easing of the Israeli movement restrictions that intensified during the second intifada, and a Palestinian Authority (PA) reform program. By 2012, however, foreign budget support had declined by more than half, and gross domestic product (GDP) growth has fallen from 9 percent in 2008–11 to 5.9 percent by 2012 and to 1.9 percent in the first half of 2013 (with negative growth of -0.1 percent in the West Bank).

This slowdown has exposed the distorted nature of the economy and its artificial reliance on donor-financed consumption. For a small open economy, prosperity requires a strong tradable sector with the ability to compete in the global marketplace. The faltering nature of the peace process and the persistence of administrative restrictions as well as others on trade, movement, and access have had a dampening effect on private investment and private sector activity. Private investment has averaged a mere 15 percent of GDP over the past seven years, compared with rates of over 25 percent in vigorous middle-income countries.

The manufacturing sector, usually a key driver of export-led growth, has stagnated since 1994, its share in GDP falling from 19 percent to 10 percent by 2011. Nor has manufacturing been replaced by high value-added service exports like Information Technology (IT) or tourism, as might have been expected. Much of the meager investment has been channeled into internal trade and real estate development, neither of which generates significant employment. Consequently, unemployment rates have remained very high in the Palestinian territories and are currently about 22 percent—with almost a quarter of the workforce employed by the Palestinian Authority, an unhealthy proportion that reflects the lack of dynamism in the private sector. While the unsettled political environment and internal Palestinian political divisions have contributed to investor aversion to the Palestinian territories, Israeli restrictions on trade, movement, and access have been seen as the dominant deterrent.

Area C is key to future Palestinian economic development. The decisive negative economic impact of Israeli restrictions has been analyzed in many reports produced by the World Bank and other development agencies over the past decade, and Israel's rationale for them—that they are necessary to protect Israeli citizens—is also well known. Within this setting, Area C is particularly important because it is either off limits for Palestinian economic activity, or only accessible with considerable difficulty and often at prohibitive cost. Since Area C is where the majority of the West Bank's natural resources lie, the impact of these restrictions on the Palestinian economy has been considerable. Thus, the key to Palestinian prosperity continues to lie in the removal of these restrictions with due regard for Israel's security. As this report shows, rolling back the restrictions would bring substantial benefits to the Palestinian economy and could usher in a new period of increasing Palestinian GDP and substantially improved prospects for sustained growth.

This report examines the economic benefits of lifting the restrictions on movement and access as well as other administrative obstacles to Palestinian investment and economic activity in Area C. It focuses on the economic potential of Area C and does not prejudge the status of any territory which may be subject to negotiations between Palestinians and Israelis. We examine potential direct, sector-specific benefits, but also indirect benefits related to improvements in physical and institutional infrastructure, as well as spillover effects to other sectors of the Palestinian economy. The sectors we examine are agriculture, Dead Sea minerals exploitation, stone mining and quarrying, construction, tourism, telecommunications, and cosmetics. To do so, we have assumed that the various physical, legal, regulatory, and bureaucratic constraints that currently prevent investors from obtaining construction permits, and accessing land and water resources are lifted, as envisaged under the Interim Agreement. We then estimate potential production and value added, using deliberately conservative assumptions—and avoid quantification where data are inadequate (as with cosmetics, for example, or for tourism other than that of Dead Sea resorts). It is understood that realizing the full potential of such investments requires other changes as well—first, the rolling back of the movement and access restrictions in force outside Area C, which

Executive Summary

prevent the easy export of Palestinian products and inhibit tourists and investors from accessing Area C; and second, further reforms by the Palestinian Authority to better enable potential investors to register businesses, enforce contracts, and acquire finance.

Direct Benefits

Neglecting indirect positive effects, we estimate that the potential additional output from the sectors evaluated in this report alone would amount to at least USD 2.2 billion per annum in valued-added terms—a sum equivalent to 23 percent of 2011 Palestinian GDP.[4] The bulk of this would come from agriculture and Dead Sea minerals exploitation.

- In the case of **agriculture**, the key issues are access to fertile land, and the availability of water to irrigate it. We have omitted from our calculations the 187,000 dunums that fall under the control of Israeli settlements. To irrigate the 326,400 dunums of other agricultural land notionally available to Palestinians in Area C would require some 189 MCM of water per year. Current Palestinian allocations under the Oslo Accords are 138.5 MCM, or 20 percent of the estimated availability—a share to be revisited at Final Status negotiations. Irrigating this unexploited area as well as accessing additional range and forest land could deliver an additional USD 704 million in value added to the Palestinian economy—equivalent to 7 percent of 2011 GDP.
- The Dead Sea abounds in valuable **minerals**, principally large deposits of potash and bromine. Israel and Jordan together derive some USD 4.2 billion in annual sales of these products, and account for 6 percent of the world's supply of potash and fully 73 percent of global bromine output. Demand for both these products is projected to remain strong, with the Dead Sea a cheap and easily exploited source. There is no reason to suppose that Palestinian investors along with prospective international partners would not be able to reap the benefits of this market, provided they were able to access the resource. Taking as a benchmark the average value added by these industries to the Jordanian and the Israeli economies, the Palestinian economy could derive up to USD 918 million per annum—equal to 9 percent of 2011 GDP, almost equivalent to the size of the entire Palestinian manufacturing sector.
- Area C is also rich in stone, with estimated deposits of some 20,000 dunums of quarryable land. Palestinian **stone mining and quarrying** is already Palestinian territories' largest export industry with exports based on the famous "Jerusalem Gold Stone." However, this is a struggling industry, due to an inability to obtain permits to open new quarries, and with most existing quarries in Area C unable to renew their licenses. If these restrictions are lifted, we estimate that the industry could double in size, increasing value added by some USD 241 million—and adding 2 percent to 2011 Palestinian GDP.
- The **construction** industry is in acute need of additional land to expand housing and make it more affordable. Areas A and B are already very densely

populated and built up. United Nations Office for the Coordination of Humanitarian Affairs (UNOCHA) analysis suggests that less than 1 percent of the land in Area C is currently available to Palestinians for construction; permit data also show that it is almost impossible to obtain permission to build in Area C. Less than 6 percent of all requests made between 2000 and 2007 secured approval. This situation applies not only to housing but also to public economic infrastructure (roads, water reservoirs, waste treatment plants) and industrial plant, and to the access roads and utility lines needed to connect Areas A and B across Area C. These factors have led to much suppressed growth in the construction sector and to an average increase in housing prices in the West Bank over the past two decades that is some 24 percent above what would otherwise be expected. We estimate that lifting the tight restrictions on the construction of residential and commercial buildings alone (excluding infrastructure projects) could increase West Bank construction sector value added by some USD 239 million per annum—or 2 percent of 2011 Palestinian GDP.

- Area C has major global *tourism* potential, but for Palestinians this remains largely unexploited due to a large degree to current restrictions on access and investment, in particular around the Dead Sea. Palestinian Dead Sea tourism development was envisaged in the Interim Agreement, but has not yet emerged. If current restrictions are lifted and investment climate in the West Bank improves, it is reasonable to assume that, in due course, Palestinian investors would be able to create a Dead Sea hotel industry equivalent to Israel's, producing value added of some USD 126 million per annum—or 1 percent of 2011 Palestinian GDP. Investments to develop other attractive tourism locations in Area C could generate substantial additional revenues.
- The development of the Palestinian *telecommunications* sector is also constrained by Area C restrictions, which prevent the construction of towers for mobile service and have impeded the laying of landlines and asymmetric digital subscriber line (ADSL) cable. Only limited 2G frequencies have been provided to the two Palestinian mobile operators, while access to the 3G spectrum has not been granted at all. Importation of equipment has also been difficult. As a result, Palestinian telecommunications costs are high, and coverage and service quality are less than optimal. The 3G restrictions in particular threaten the industry's very viability, particularly since Israeli competitors have been allowed to develop infrastructure in Area C. We estimate that removing today's restrictions would not only remove a serious threat to the viability of this industry but also add some USD 48 million in value to the sector—equal to 0.5 percent of Palestinian 2011 GDP.

Indirect Benefits

In addition to the direct benefits discussed in chapter 2, the indirect benefits of removing the restrictions in Area C would be significant. Indirect costs and benefits can be divided into those related to physical and institutional infrastructure, and spillover-related costs and benefits. The first set of costs and benefits are driven by the impact of Israeli restrictions on the *quality* and *cost* of infrastructure; the impact of the restrictions in this instance is difficult to measure, and no attempt to do so is made here. Nonetheless, the effects are considerable and are alluded to below. The spillover effects derive first from the fact that sectors are linked, with one using the outputs of another as production inputs—and those effects can be quantified. In addition, there is also a spillover effect (that is, induced effect) generated when additional income generated by new activities is spent to purchase on goods and services. Induced effect has not been quantified either.

The quality and cost of infrastructure are impacted considerably by the restrictions present in Area C. All Palestinian industries are to some extent dependent on the quality of transportation, electricity, water, and telecommunications infrastructure. Transportation infrastructure is particularly problematic as Palestinian use of roads in Area C is highly restricted, and travel times can be inordinate; the Palestinian Authority has also been unable to develop roads, airports, or railways in or through Area C. Restrictions in Area C have impeded the development of "soft" institutional infrastructure such as banking services, which are hamstrung by the inability to open and service branches, and the inability in practice to use land in Area C as collateral. Insecurity and the difficulty of policing Area C also deter investors. These impediments create significant uncertainty and reduce the expected returns on potential investments.

Addressing the constraints on the evaluated sectors would have sizeable effects on the demand for output in other related sectors. Despite the relative lack of diversification of the Palestinian economy and the undeveloped nature of its domestic supply chains, these linkages are important. The potential spillover effects for the rest of the Palestinian economy emanating from the expansion of these sectors were calculated by using data on intersectoral linkages produced recently by the Palestinian Central Bureau of Statistics. The overall multiplier effect emerging from this exercise is 1.5—a figure calculated without reliance on a general equilibrium model, and very probably an underestimate.[5] Applying this multiplier, the total potential value added from alleviating today's restrictions on access to, and activity and production in Area C is likely to amount to some USD 3.4 billion—or 35 percent of Palestinian GDP in 2011, as illustrated in the figure ES.1 below.

Tapping this potential output could dramatically improve the PA's fiscal position. Even without any improvements in the efficiency of tax collection, at the current rate of tax/GDP of 20 percent the additional tax revenues associated with such an increase in GDP would amount to some USD 800 million (figure ES.2). Assuming that expenditures remain at the same level, this extra resource would notionally cut the fiscal deficit by half—significantly reducing the need for donor recurrent budget support.[6] This major improvement in fiscal sustainability would in turn generate significant positive reputational benefits for the PA and would considerably enhance investor confidence.

Figure ES.1 Growth Generated Through the Lifting of Restrictions Could Increase Potential Palestinian Value Added by USD 3.4 Billion

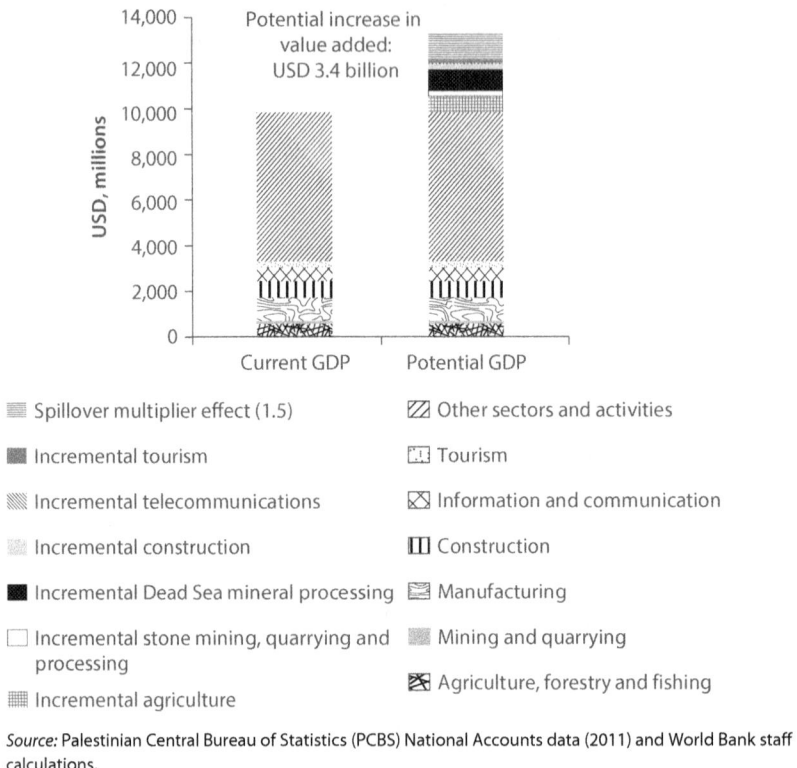

Source: Palestinian Central Bureau of Statistics (PCBS) National Accounts data (2011) and World Bank staff calculations.
Note: GDP = gross domestic product; USD = United States dollars.

The impact on Palestinian livelihoods would be impressive. An increase in GDP equivalent to 35 percent would be expected to create substantial employment, sufficient to put a significant dent in the currently high rate of unemployment. If an earlier-estimated one-to-one relationship between growth and employment was to hold, this increase in GDP would lead to a 35 percent increase in employment. This level of growth in employment would also put a large dent in poverty, as recent estimates show that unemployed Palestinians are twice as likely to be poor as their employed counterparts.

Access to Area C will not cure all Palestinian economic problems—but the alternative is bleak. Without the ability to conduct purposeful economic activity in Area C, the economic space of the West Bank will remain crowded and stunted, inhabited by people whose daily interactions with the State of Israel are characterized by inconvenience, expense, and frustration.

Figure ES.2 If the Output Potential Associated with Lifting the Restrictions Materializes, the Fiscal Deficit of the PA Is Reduced by 56 Percent and the Need for External Budget Support Greatly Declines

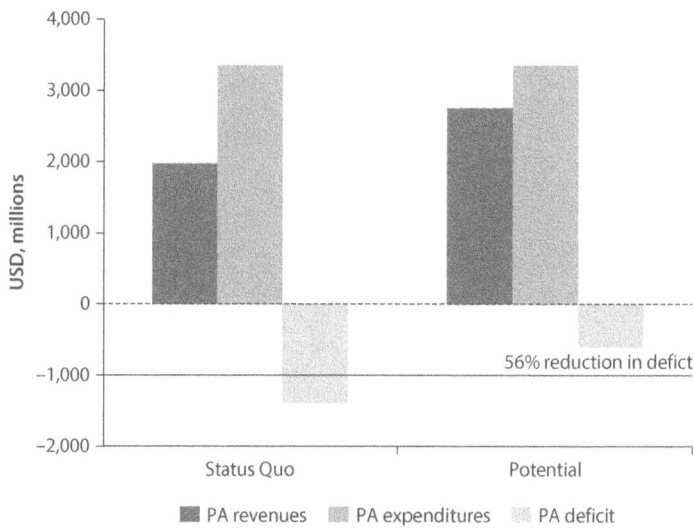

Source: Ministry of Finance of Palestinian authority fiscal data (2012) and World Bank staff calculations.
Note: PA = Palestinian Authority; USD = United States dollars.

Notes

1. The 1995 Israeli-Palestinian Interim Agreement on the West Bank and Gaza Strip, Article XI, Para 3(c).

2. See Interim Agreement Article XI, para 2(d) according to which the redeployment of the Israeli military forces from the West Bank and Gaza, except for issues that will be negotiated in the permanent status negotiations, should have been completed within 18 months from the date of the inauguration of the Palestinian Legislative Council which took place on March 7, 1996.

3. The Wye River Memorandum signed between the Palestinian Liberation Organization and the Government of Israel on October 23, 1998 included further arrangements regarding Israeli redeployment from Area C. However, the implementation of the Memorandum was very limited and only 2 percent of Area C was transferred to the status of Area B.

4. Sensitivity of these estimates to different assumptions on key variables is shown in appendix A.

5. A general equilibrium model would capture third-round effects, the effects of infrastructure development in Area C, and other indirect effects, which our calculation did not capture. Such a model would also capture price effects, which in the short and medium term would have a negative impact on demand, but would adjust in the long run, which allows for capacity adjustments.

6. In reality, the lifting of restrictions on Area C would probably lead to an increase in public investments to develop infrastructure there. These investments would increase public expenditures, but they would also contribute to growth and the net effect is uncertain. Thus, for the sake of this report no change in the level of public expenditures associated with the lifting of Area C restrictions was assumed.

CHAPTER 1

The Palestinian Economy, Israeli Restrictions, and the Potential of Area C

The Palestinian Economy: Volatility, Distorted Growth, and Uncertain Prospects

Palestinian economic growth since 1994 has been volatile and unpredictable as illustrated by figure 1.1. The Oslo peace process and the establishment of the Palestinian Authority (PA) ushered in an era of rapid growth, driven by the return of the Palestinian Diaspora, periods of relative tranquility and large inflows of public and private capital. Average real gross domestic product (GDP) increased by 8.4 percent per annum between 1994 and 1999. The outbreak of the second Intifada in 2000 interrupted this trend, bringing increased violence and uncertainty—and most significantly, the intensification by Israel of a complex set of security-related restrictions that impeded the movement of people and goods and fragmented the Palestinian territories into small enclaves lacking economic cohesion. In the ensuing recession, GDP contracted by an average of 9 percent per annum in 2000–02. An initial period of recovery was interrupted by the turmoil surrounding the internal divide between Fatah and Hamas in mid-2007 before a sustained period of growth between 2007 and 2011, in which Palestinian reforms were accompanied by large inflows of donor assistance and some easing of movement restrictions.

Recent growth rates are proving unsustainable, however. Growth in recent years has been driven largely by extraordinary levels of donor budget support, which amounted to USD 1.8 billion, or 29 percent of GDP, in 2008. This fuelled a significant expansion in consumption, particularly the consumption of valuable public services such as policing, education, and health (the share of public administration, education, and health care in GDP increased from 19 to 26 percent between 1994 and 2011). By 2012, however, budget support had decreased by more than half, and growth rates had declined from 9 percent in 2008–11 to 5.9 percent by 2012 and 1.9 percent in the first half of 2013 (–0.1 percent in the West Bank).

The reduction in budget support and the resultant contraction in Palestinian growth have exposed the distorted nature of the Palestinian economy. For a small

Figure 1.1 Real GDP Growth Rate 1999–First Half 2013

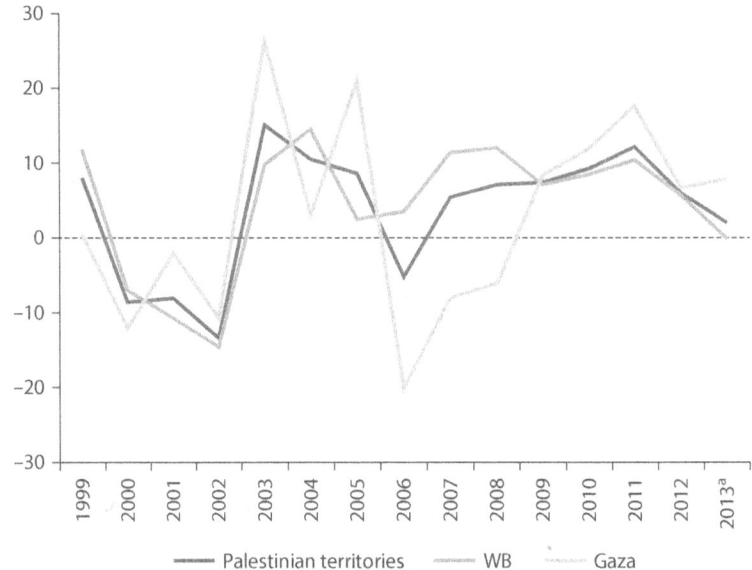

Source: Palestinian Central Bureau of Statistics (PCBS) National Accounts data.
Note: GDP = gross domestic product; WB = World Bank.
a. Based on preliminary data for the first half of 2013.

open economy, prosperity requires a strong tradable sector with the ability to compete in the global marketplace. The faltering nature of the peace process and the persistence of restrictions on trade, movement, and access have had a dampening effect on private investment and private sector activity. The manufacturing sector, usually a key driver of export-led growth, has stagnated since 1994, its share in GDP falling from 19 percent to 10 percent by 2011 (Figure 1.2). Nor has manufacturing been replaced by high value-added service exports like Information Technology (IT) or tourism, as might have been expected. Stagnation and declining competitiveness are also apparent in the agriculture sector where employment doubled from 53,000 in 1995 to 99,000 in 2011 while productivity, or output per worker, declined by half.

Private investment rates have remained low, with the bulk channeled into relatively unproductive activities that generate insufficient employment. Private investment has averaged around 15 percent of GDP over the past seven years, as compared with rates of over 25 percent in fast-growing middle-income economies, and with foreign direct investment (FDI) averaging a mere 1 percent of GDP, which is also very low in comparison to most fast-growing economies. Much of this investment is also channeled into internal trade and real estate development, neither of which generates significant employment. Consequently, unemployment rates have remained very high in the Palestinian territories. After initial post-Oslo rates of about 9 percent in the mid-1990s, unemployment rose to 28 percent of the labor force in 2000 with the onset of the second intifada and the imposition of severe movement and access restrictions; it has remained high

Figure 1.2 The Decline in the Tradable Sectors

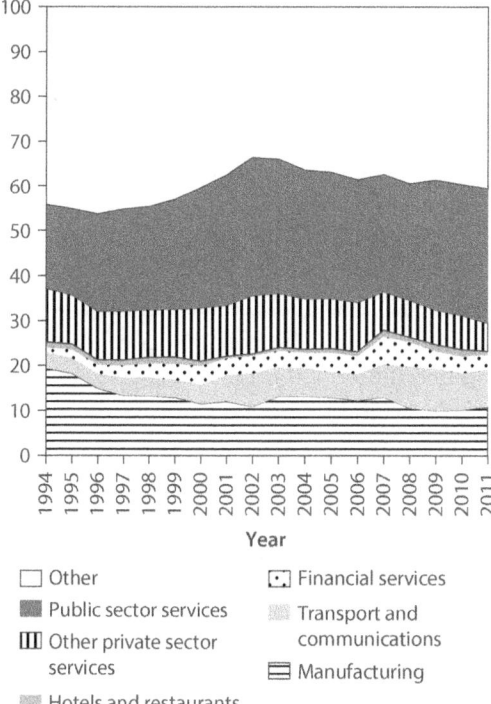

Source: Palestinian Central Bureau of Statistics (PCBS) National Accounts data.

ever since and is currently about 22 percent.[1] What is more, almost 24 percent of the workforce is employed by the PA, an uncommonly high proportion that reflects the lack of dynamism in the private sector. While internal Palestinian political divisions have contributed to investor aversion to the Palestinian territories, Israeli restrictions on trade, movement, and access are clearly the binding constraint to investment: these restrictions substantially increase the cost of trade and make it impossible to import many production inputs into the Palestinian territories, as illustrated, for instance, on the example of the telecommunications sector. For Gaza, the restrictions on import and export are in particular severe. In addition to the restrictions on labor movement between the Palestinian territories, the restrictions on movement of labor within the West Bank have been shown to have a strong impact on employability, wages, and economic growth. Israeli restrictions render much economic activity very difficult or impossible to conduct on about 61 percent of the West Bank territory, called Area C.

Restrictions on Movement and Access, and the Stunted Potential of Area C

The complex system of restrictions on movement and access imposed by Israel is the most significant impediment to Palestinian private sector growth. The decisive economic impact of Israeli restrictions has been analyzed in many Bank reports and reports prepared by other development agencies over the past decade, and Israel's rationale for them—that they are necessary to protect Israeli citizens—is also well known. The movement of people and goods into and out of the Palestinian territories, and within the West Bank, is severely limited by a multi-layered system of physical, institutional, and administrative impediment.[2] Physical barriers are compounded by unpredictable regulatory measures and practices—notably the large list of "dual-use"[3] items that cannot be imported because Israel regards them as a security risk—and by limited access to water and to the electromagnetic spectrum.

Restrictions on economic activity specific to Area C of the West Bank have been particularly detrimental to the Palestinian economy. The potential contribution of Area C to the Palestinian economy is enormous. It constitutes about 61 percent of the West Bank[4] and is home to around 180,000 Palestinian people, or approximately 6.6 percent of the Palestinian West Bank population.[5]

It is richly endowed with natural resources; and it is contiguous, whereas Areas A and B are territorial islands (table 1.1). The manner in which Area C is currently administered virtually precludes Palestinian businesses from investing there. Relieving these restrictions would have substantial positive effects on the Palestinian economy, as chapters 2 and 3 will demonstrate.

The division of the West Bank into Areas A, B, and C dates back to the 1995 Interim Agreement between the Palestinian Liberation Organization and the Government of Israel. Area A includes most major preexisting Palestinian urban areas, covers 18 percent of the West Bank, and is under full Palestinian security and civil control. Area B consists largely of peri-urban areas and small towns, comprises 21 percent of the West Bank, and is under Palestinian civil control and Israeli security control.[6] Area C was defined under the Interim Agreement as "areas of the West Bank outside Areas A and B, which, except for the issues that will be negotiated in the permanent status negotiations, will be gradually transferred to Palestinian jurisdiction in accordance with this Agreement."[7] According to the

Table 1.1 Significance of Area C in Terms of Natural Resources

Natural resource	In Area A	In Area B	In Area C	Natural resource in Area C as a percentage of total in West Bank (%)
Nature reserves (dunums[a])	52,300	42,600	607,730	86
Forests (dunums)	7,000	9,000	59,016	91
Wells	223	87	287[b]	48
Springs	70	122	112	37

Source: Applied Research Institute in Jerusalem (ARIJ), 2013.
a. 1 dunum is approximately equal to 0.25 acre.
b. The figure for Area C is relatively low and its value can probably be attributed to Area C restrictions, which preclude the exploration and opening of new wells in Area C. Thus, it is probable that this figure significantly underestimates the true number of wells in the Area.

Interim Agreement, the gradual transfer should have been completed by 1997.[8] However, it has not been implemented as envisaged in the Interim Agreement.[9]

Only a very small part of Area C is accessible to Palestinian economic agents, and is fully subject to Israeli military control.[10] Less than 1 percent of Area C, which is already built up, is designated by the Israeli authorities for Palestinian use; the remainder is heavily restricted or off-limits to Palestinians,[11] with 68 percent reserved for Israeli settlements,[12] c. 21 percent for closed military zones,[13] and c. 9 percent for nature reserves (approximately 10 percent of the West Bank, 86 percent of which lies in Area C). These areas are not mutually exclusive, and overlap in some cases. In practice it is virtually impossible for Palestinians to obtain construction permits for residential or economic purposes, even within existing Palestinian villages in Area C: The application process has been described by an earlier World Bank report (2008) as fraught with "ambiguity, complexity and high cost."[14] The same is true for the extraction of natural resources and development of public infrastructure.

The proportion of Area C available for Palestinian economic development is being constricted by the expansion of Israeli settlements. The Israeli settler population in the West Bank grew from 111,600 in 1993 to 328,423 by 2011, and the proportion of Area C devoted to their settlements has expanded rapidly.[15] Settlement areas grew by 35 percent between 2000 and 2011 and now cover almost 3.25 percent of the West Bank.[16] The territory actually controlled by settlements far exceeds this, and according to Israeli sources amounts to fully 68 percent of Area C.[17] In addition to built-up areas, this includes the settlements' municipal boundaries, development master plan areas, and road networks, all of which are usually off limits to Palestinians. Reports by the Israeli Ministry of Defense in 2012 further state that an additional 10 percent of Area C has been earmarked for settlement expansion.[18] The perceived need to protect Israeli settlers is seen by some observers as the key driver behind many of the restrictions imposed on Palestinians in Area C.[19]

Much fuller Palestinian economic access to Area C, as envisaged in the Interim Agreement, would—if accompanied by a major reduction in general movement and access restrictions—have a decisive impact on Palestinian economic prospects. The paper will illustrate this by estimating the economic costs to the Palestinian economy of today's restrictions, and the potential benefits of relieving them and it does not prejudge the status of any territory which may be subject to negotiations between Palestinians and Israelis. Chapter 2 will look at the direct costs to the two sectors with the greatest upside potential—agriculture, and Dead Sea minerals production—and will also reference the income foregone in stone mining and quarrying, construction, tourism, and telecommunications. Chapter 3 will then calculate the indirect benefits that could accrue to the Palestinian economy as a whole from an expansion of Palestinian economic activity in Area C. As will become clear, these benefits not only include a significant reduction in unemployment and the prospect of vigorous levels of private sector-led growth but also would lead to a significant reduction of current Palestinian dependence on donor-financed budget support. It is understood that a drastic rollback of

Box 1.1 Limited Access to Education for Palestinians Who Live in Area C Increases Their Chance of Being Poor

An example which illustrates the vulnerability of communities falling in Area C directly relates to the lack of basic services. The map below plots the most frequent level of education reported by heads of household for each locality. A few pockets of high levels of average education (higher than secondary) are plotted in blue and also correspond to localities with low levels of poverty. In contrast, localities where many heads of household have primary education or less (in pink) are on average more likely to be very poor. The latter are predominantly in the eastern part of the West Bank, overlapping with Area C, where access to education services may be very limited.

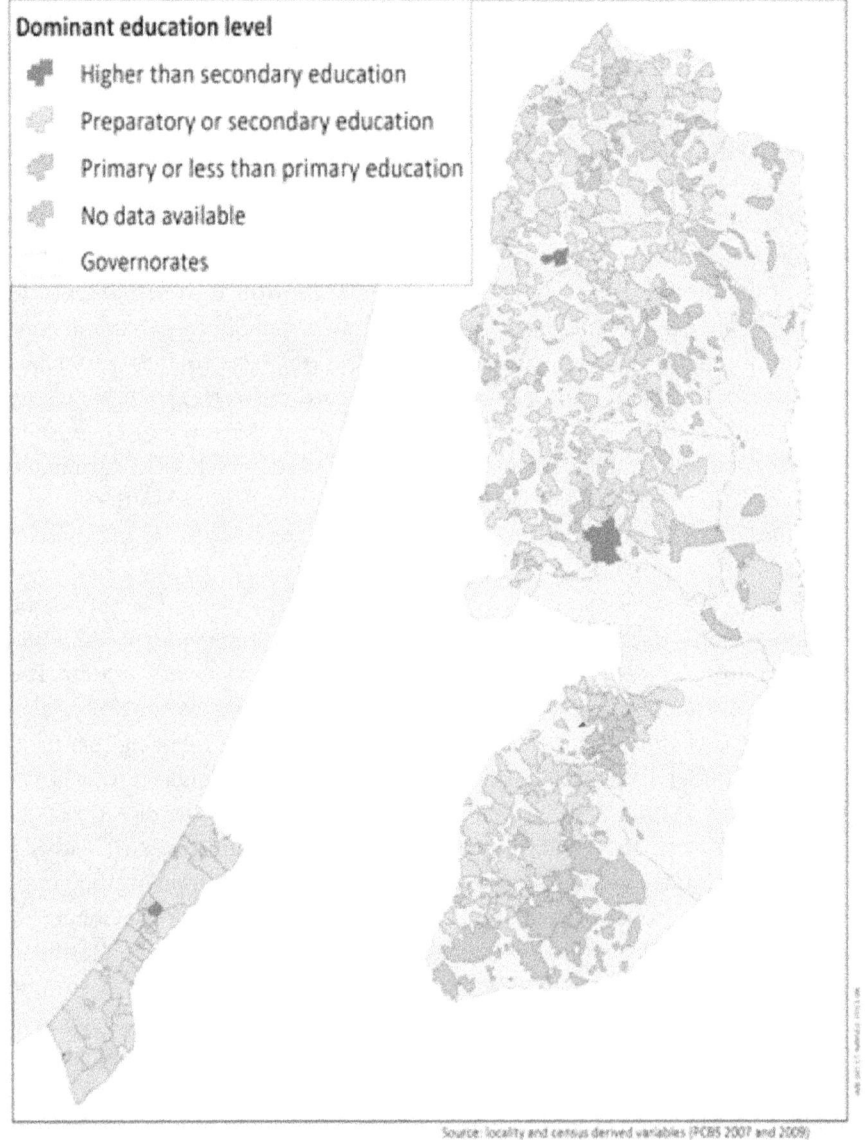

Source: locality and census derived variables (PCBS 2007 and 2009)

today's regime of movement and access restrictions is likely to require a new and more positive bilateral dynamic between Israel and the Palestinians, which will among other things address the Israeli security concerns.

Notes

1. The overall unemployment figure for WBG masks significant regional divergences. Unemployment in the West Bank stood at 19 percent in the first half of 2013 compared to 30 percent in Gaza.
2. Access to Gaza remains highly controlled, and only consumer goods and construction material for donor-supervised projects are allowed in. Exports from Gaza to the West Bank and Israeli markets, traditionally Gaza's main export destinations, are prohibited (according to Gisha, an Israeli nonprofit organization founded in 2005 to protect the freedom of movement of Palestinians, especially Gaza residents, 85 percent of Gaza products were exported to Israel and the West Bank prior to 2007, at which point Israeli restrictions were tightened). The only shipments of agricultural and manufactured products exiting Gaza to third country markets today are negligible amounts exported under the aegis of donor-financed projects.
3. The "dual-use" list contains goods, raw materials, and equipment that in addition to their civilian use could be used for military purposes, and therefore cannot be imported by Palestinian businesses. Dual-use trade restrictions are not uncommon internationally and may serve legitimate security concerns. However, the list of dual-use items whose import to West Bank and Gaza is banned by Government of Israel (GoI) is unusually extensive. These restrictions raise the cost of inputs and force Palestinian businesses to use inefficient input mixes—and in some cases, to drop product lines. Most Palestinian industries are affected by the dual-use list—particularly food and beverages, pharmaceuticals, textiles, information technology, agriculture, and metal processing. The "dual-use" list does not apply to Israeli importers. It is reported that Palestinian businesses can sometimes procure these goods from Israeli businesses.
4. The vague definition of Area C in the Interim Agreement made it difficult to identify its exact boundaries; consequently Area C has come to be defined as all West Bank territory that is not part of Areas A and B.
5. The Area C population figure comes from personal communications with Bimkom, an Israeli nonprofit organization. This figure is not precise because data for the distribution of population between Area C and Areas A and B are not available, and since two-thirds of towns and villages fall partly in Area C and partly in Areas A and B.
6. World Bank Ad Hoc Liaison Committee (AHLC) Report, September 2008. "Palestinian Economic Prospects: Aid, Access, and Reform."
7. The 1995 Israeli-Palestinian Interim Agreement on the West Bank and Gaza Strip Article XI, para 3(c); available on the Israeli Ministry of Foreign Affairs website: http://www.mfa.gov.il/MFA/Peace+Process/Guide+to+the+Peace+Process/THE+ISRAELI-PALESTINIAN+INTERIM+AGREEMENT+-+Annex+VI.htm.
8. See Interim Agreement Article XI, para 2(d) according to which the redeployment of the Israeli military forces from the West Bank and Gaza, except for issues that will be negotiated in the permanent status negotiations, should have been completed within 18 months from the date of the inauguration of the Palestinian Legislative Council which took place on March 7, 1996.

9. The Wye River Memorandum signed between the Palestinian Liberation Organization and the Government of Israel on October 23, 1998, included further arrangements regarding Israeli redeployment from Area C. However, the implementation of the memorandum was very limited and only 2 percent of Area C was transferred to the status of Area B.
10. The Israeli Civil Administration, subordinate to Israeli Defense Force's Coordinator of Government Activities in the Territories, or COGAT, administers civilian affairs in the West Bank.
11. United Nations Office for the Coordination of Humanitarian Affairs (OCHA), 2009. "Restricting Space: The Planning Regime Applied by Israel in Area C of the West Bank."
12. Much of the territory controlled by the settlements is land that has been declared by the Israeli government to be "state land," through the application of the Ottoman Land Law—and this includes land which Israel also considers to be private Palestinian land. B'tselem found that 21 percent of the built-up area of the settlements is classified as Palestinian private property—see B'tselem, 2010. "By Hook and by Crook: Israeli Settlement Policy in the West Bank." See also B'tselem, 2011. "Taking Control of Land." Published on http://www.btselem.org/.
13. These include areas allocated to military training, military bases, secured areas around settlements, land between the West Bank Separation Barrier and the Green Line, and a security strip along the Jordanian border—see OCHA, 2009, op. cit.
14. World Bank. 2008. "The Economic Effects of Restricted Access to Land in the West Bank." The complexity of the procedures is mainly attributed to GoI suspension of planning and land registration in 1968, which made it difficult and costly to prove ownership.
15. Source of data for settlement population: Foundation for Middle East Peace.
16. The Applied Research Institute in Jerusalem (ARIJ) database, 2012.
17. B'tselem, 2010. "By Hook and By Crook: Israeli Settlement Policy in the West Bank." The total area of the West Bank is approximately 5.661 million dunums, or 1.398 million acres.
18. Haaretz, March 30, 2012. Found at: http://www.haaretz.com/news/diplomacy-defense/israel-defense-ministry-plan-earmarks-10-percent-of-west-bank-for-settlement-expansion-1.421589.
19. See for example World Bank, 2007. "Movement and Access Restrictions in the West Bank: Uncertainty and Inefficiency in the Palestinian Economy."

CHAPTER 2

Area C—Output Potential of Key Sectors of the Palestinian Economy

The alleviation of today's restrictions on Palestinian investment, movement and access in Area C could bring about significant expansion of many sectors of the Palestinian economy. This chapter examines the direct impact of the restrictions—and the benefits of alleviating them—for a number of important sectors of the Palestinian economy. Relatively conservative estimates show that the direct gains, in terms of potential value added in these sectors, would amount to at least USD 2.2 billion, equivalent to some 23 percent of 2011 Palestinian gross domestic product (GDP).

Agriculture

West Bank agriculture's contribution to the Palestinian economy is declining. As figure 2.1 shows, agriculture contributed over 14 percent of West Bank GDP in

Figure 2.1 Agriculture Value Added in the West Bank
constant 2004 USD million, percentage of GDP

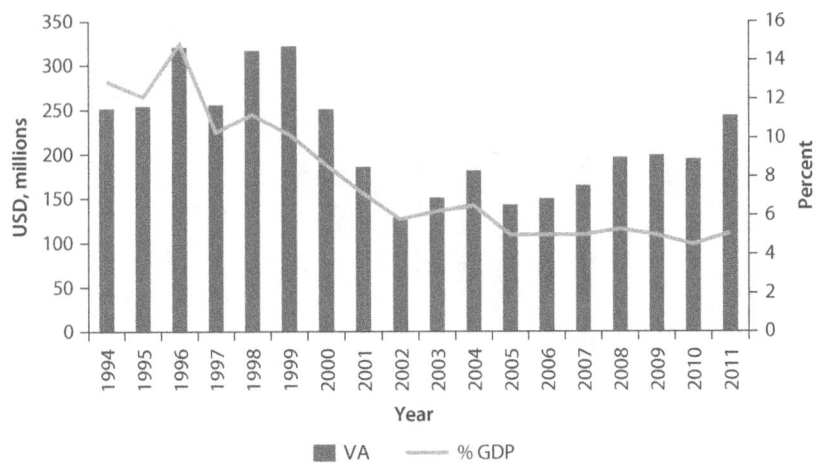

Source: Palestinian Central Bureau of Statistics (PCBS) (2012a).
Note: GDP = gross domestic product; USD = United States dollars; VA = value added.

the mid-1990s, but only 5.1 percent in 2011. Real value added has also fallen considerably from its 1999 peak.

At the same time, though, the number of West Bankers employed in agriculture more than doubled between 1995 and 2006 (Figure 2.2). The decreasing importance of agriculture has not been accompanied by any corresponding movement of workers out of agriculture into more productive sectors, as would be typical in a modernizing economy.[1]

Consequently, agricultural labor productivity in the West Bank is in significant decline. This trend has been particularly apparent since the end of the 1990s, as figure 2.3 demonstrates. The decline is even more striking when compared to the rest of the West Bank economy—as the blue line in the figure shows, the ratio of labor productivity in agriculture relative to the economy as a whole fell by more than 50 percent between 1995 and 2011. The wage dynamics in the West Bank show that this productivity decline has meant a reduction in agricultural earnings relative to work in the economy as a whole.[2]

These abnormal trends are explained by the various restrictions on Palestinian access to and investment in the land and water resources of the West Bank, predominantly those restrictions operating in Area C. The fact that workers have not abandoned agriculture and that the sector has not witnessed any appreciable intensification speaks to the difficulties of developing alternative economic activities as well as to the limitations placed on agriculture itself. As discussed below, these restrictions impede access to large swathes of fertile land and essential water sources as well as constrain the development of the infrastructure needed for modern market-oriented agriculture.

Figure 2.2 Share of Agriculture in Total Employment, West Bank

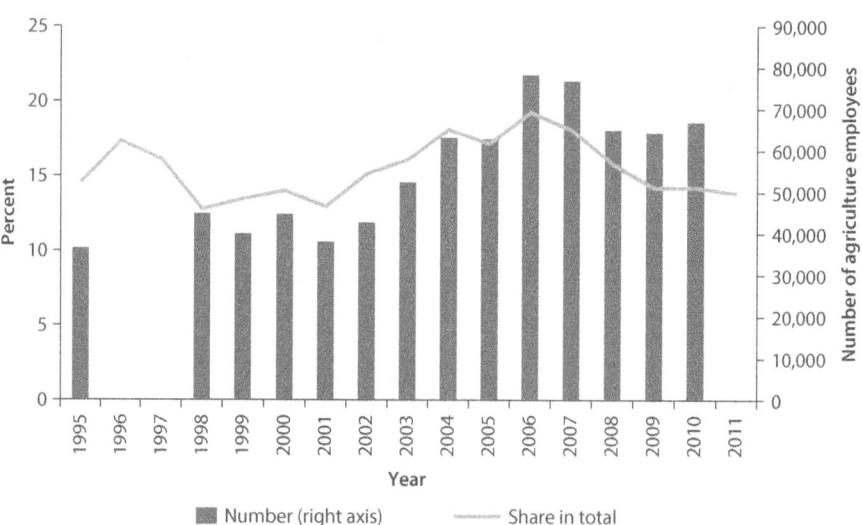

Source: PCBS Labour Force surveys (various years).
Note: The share is calculated for the residents of the West Bank whose place of work is the West Bank (workers in Israeli settlements or in Israel are excluded).

Figure 2.3 West Bank Labor Productivity
Value added/worker, and relative to the overall economy

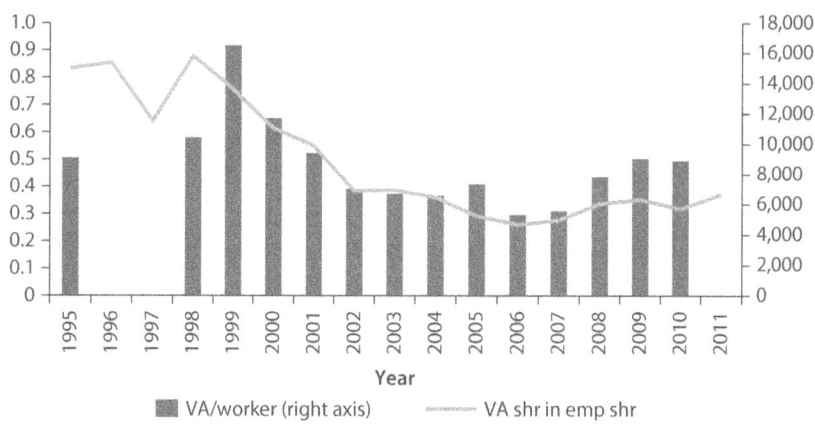

Source: PCBS (2012a) and PCBS Labor Force surveys (various years).
Note: The sampling weights are not correct in the Labor Force surveys for 1996 and 1997, which prevents the computation of the VA/worker in those years. VA = value added.

Area C Restrictions and the Decline of Palestinian Agriculture

Area C includes almost all the land of the West Bank suitable for agricultural production—a delineation inherent in Interim Agreement's zoning system, in which Area C comprises the territories beyond Palestinian urban and peri-urban areas. Palestinian access to much of this land, though, is either prohibited or severely restricted, as was described in chapter 1. The Land Research Center (LRC) has estimated that almost half a million dunums of land suitable for agriculture in Area C is not cultivated by Palestinians.[3] Some of this cannot be cultivated because of restricted access[4]—LRC estimates that 187,000 dunums are cultivated or occupied by Israeli settlements—and some of it cannot be cultivated due to lack of water. In addition, another 1 million dunums could be used for rangeland or forestry were current restrictions lifted. Although of lower economic potential, this land could generate useful income, as discussed below.

While most of the West Bank's aquifer and spring water is located in Area C, Palestinians have not been able to draw their agreed allocation of 138.5 MCM per annum. There are three underground aquifers in the West Bank: the Eastern, the Western, and the North-eastern aquifers. They are either located entirely in Area C (the Eastern Aquifer) or shared with Israel (the North-eastern and Western Aquifers). Out of the 138.5 MCM annual allocation in 2011, for example, only 87 MCM was abstracted by the Palestinians.[5] Digging wells or building water conveyance and wastewater treatment and reuse infrastructures requires approval by the Israeli Civil Administration (ICA) as well as by the Joint Water Committee if Area C is implicated, which is almost always the case.[6] Selby (2013)[7] argues that these requirements have severely restricted the number of additional wells: New Palestinian wells drilled since the Oslo Agreement provide only 13 MCM per year—below the 20.5 MCM per year allocated under the

Interim Agreement for the five-year transitional period, and considerably less than the additional 70–80 MCM per year identified for Palestinian "future needs."[8] What is more, half of Palestinian wells have dried up over the last 20 years[9]—with the result that total Palestinian water production in the West Bank has dropped by 20 MCM per year since 1994. This decline has been partially offset by an increase in water purchases from Israel of over 100 percent between 1995 and 2010.[10] Even so, per capita water access has declined by more than 30 percent.[11] These restrictions on water availability limit Palestinian irrigation possibilities and thereby constrain potential agricultural production.

Aside from access to land and water, other impediments prevent Palestinian agriculture production from approaching its potential. Permission to create the infrastructure needed to intensify agricultural production—water reservoirs, feeder roads, processing facilities—has been very difficult to obtain.[12] The Separation Barrier has cut off many farmers from their agricultural fields, many of which are located in Area C.[13]

Agricultural Potential

Current restrictions on Palestinian access to and use of the land and water resources of Area C reduce both the amount of land that can be cultivated and its productivity, largely as a consequence of restricted water availability. Estimating the potential value added of removing these restrictions is difficult and would involve many arguable assumptions—so we have taken a very conservative approach based mostly on an expansion of Palestinian-irrigated land in Area C (see appendix A to this report for a more detailed discussion of the methodology used). The settlement areas are excluded from this discussion, although they exemplify the agricultural potential in Area C (see Box 2.1).

Irrigating the approximately 326,400 dunums of arable land notionally available for Palestinian cultivation in Area C would increase Palestinian Area C production by USD 1.068 billion. With potential additional rain-fed land added and current Palestinian Area C production of USD 316 million discounted, the value of annual production would increase by some USD 890 million. This would require around 189 MCM of water per year, using the current Palestinian irrigation average of 579 litres of water per year per dunum.[14] Discussing access to this additional water is beyond the scope of this book, but it should be noted that substantial investments would be necessary.

Box 2.1 Agriculture in Israeli Settlements in Area C Exemplifies the Sector's Potential in the Area

Recent estimates suggest that the area cultivated by the settlements in the West Bank has expanded rapidly, growing by 35 percent since 1997 and reaching around 93 thousand dunums in 2012. The cropping pattern of settler agriculture suggests good access to water and consequently higher productivity. In 2012, only 5 percent of the agricultural land cultivated by the settlements in the West Bank was devoted to olive production, one of the cultivations with the

box continued next page

Box 2.1 Agriculture in Israeli Settlements in Area C exemplifies the Sector's Potential in the Area *(continued)*

least water requirement. This minimal water requirement is one of the main reasons why almost half of the agricultural land cultivated by the Palestinians in the Palestinian territory is devoted to olive trees. Thus, better access to water would enable a similar shift in the cropping pattern and increased productivity of agriculture in the Palestinian economy. There is no publicly available information to estimate the value of agricultural production in Israeli settlements. A conservative estimate, which relies on the current Palestinian productivity level of irrigated land in the West Bank, suggests that the potential agricultural value of the settlements' land used for agriculture is at least USD 251 million, equivalent to USD 196 million in value added. This large potential is confirmed by the fact that the settlements currently provide most of the pomegranates exported to Europe and the Russian Federation, in addition to 22 percent of the almonds and 12.9 percent of the olives among others. The Jordan Valley settlements produce 60 percent of the dates destined to Israel and 40 percent of the exported dates.

Source: Karem Navot, 2013. "Israeli settler agriculture: as a means of land takeover in the West Bank."

Area C also contains rangeland and forests which could be exploited in the absence of access and usage restrictions. The total potential value of this rangeland, measured in terms of fodder that could be produced annually with unrestricted access, amounts to just over USD 7 million per year, of which only just over some USD 1 million is currently realized.[15] Access to forests in Area C and their sustainable exploitation would also add value to the Palestinian economy, but we lack adequate information to estimate this.

The total additional production thus amounts to USD 896 million per year. Using the 78 percent ratio of agriculture value added to output applied in the Palestinian National Accounts, this translates into USD 704 million in value added.[16] This represents 9.5 percent of West Bank GDP in 2011, and 7 percent of total 2011 Palestinian GDP, and is almost certainly an underestimate of the true figure: It concentrates almost solely on irrigated potential and uses as benchmarks levels of Palestinian production that are themselves repressed by movement and access restrictions.

Dead Sea Minerals

Proven vast mineral deposits exist in the Dead Sea, offering major potential for the Palestinian economy. As the large international corporation Israeli Chemicals, Ltd. (ICL) notes in its 2012 annual report, "The Dead Sea is a vast (practically inexhaustible) and highly concentrated source of reserves of potash, bromine, magnesium and salt."[17] Access to this resource endowment would permit the emergence of several large industrial activities based on the extraction of potash, bromine, and magnesium, as well as salts and secondary industries such as cosmetics. As yet, though, the Palestinian economy is unable to benefit from this potential due to restricted access, permit issues, and the uncertainties of the investment climate. This contrasts sharply with the experience of Israel and Jordan.

Israel and Jordan are benefiting considerably from the Dead Sea mineral endowment. Both countries have developed industries that contribute substantial value added, exports, and jobs to their two economies. Israeli companies generate around USD 3 billion annually from the sale of Dead Sea minerals (primarily potash and bromine) and from other products, which are derived from Dead Sea Minerals. Jordanian Dead Sea mineral industries are smaller but still generate about USD 1.2 billion in sales (equivalent to 4 percent of Jordan's GDP).[18] Potash extraction and processing industries alone contribute roughly USD 2.3 billion in sales earnings to the economies of Israel and Jordan, most of it in the form of foreign exchange from exports.[19] Between them, Israel and Jordan accounted in 2010 for about 6 percent of world potash production, and this capacity is growing—as is demand. The International Fertilizer Association forecasts a sharp increase in potash demand between 2012 and 2017, from about 50 to 70 million tons per year (Figure 2.4).[20]

Israel and Jordan also account for some 73 percent of global bromine production, all of it from the Dead Sea. While the deposits of bromine in China (the third largest producer) are being depleted, the Dead Sea offers a "virtually inexhaustible" source, according to ICL: "Due to the high concentration of bromine in the Dead Sea, bromine production is the easiest, most economically feasible and stable in the world."[21] Continued growth of the Dead Sea bromine industry is almost guaranteed, as the global demand is growing while alternative supply sources are very limited (Figure 2.5)[22].

Potential for Developing Dead Sea Minerals

The Palestinian economy could benefit enormously if it were able to attract the investment needed to develop mineral processing industries comparable to those in Jordan

Figure 2.4 Potash Price and Demand Projections, 2012–25

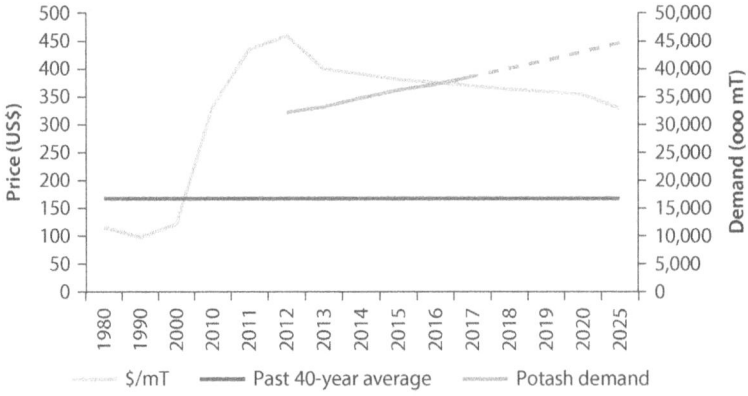

Source: World Bank Development Prospects Group, "Commodity Price Forecast Update," and Food and Agriculture Organization (FAO) of the United Nations, "Current World Fertilizer Trends and Outlook to 2016."
Note: FAO appears to significantly underestimate potash demand, as its estimate is roughly 25 percent lower than the industry estimates available in different sources. Potash demand forecast beyond 2016 is a staff estimate, assuming annual growth beyond 2016 equal to average annual growth between 2012 and 2016.

Figure 2.5 World Production of Bromine
In metric tons

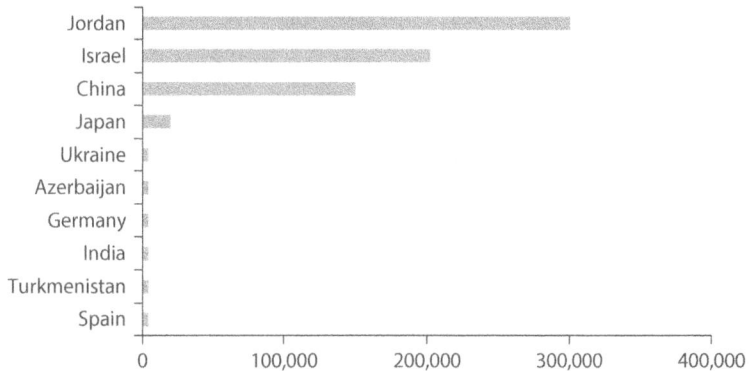

Source: Based on 2011 data found on http://www.indexmundi.com/en/commodities/minerals/bromine/bromine_t6.html.

and Israel. As unequivocally argued by ICL in its annual report, access to the Dead Sea mineral resources is the key competitive advantage in the potash and bromine industries: "The ability to compete in the market is dependent mainly on production costs and logistics."[23] According to ICL, the scale of requisite investment is the main barrier to entry into the potash market, but given the availability of cost-effective and enormous reserves, this barrier should not be insurmountable to Palestinian entrepreneurs and their potential foreign business partners.

The potential incremental value added to the Palestinian economy from the production and sales of potash, bromine, and magnesium has been conservatively estimated at USD 918 million per annum, or 9 percent of GDP. This is almost equivalent to the contribution of the entire manufacturing sector of Palestinian territories today. In calculating this figure, we have taken the average of the value added generated in Israel and in Jordan for these three products and their derivatives (see appendix A for methodological detail). We estimate that potash could generate around USD 642 million in value added, and bromine/magnesium another USD 276 million.

Stone Mining and Quarrying

Stone mining and quarrying is the largest Palestinian industry. It contributes about 15,000 jobs and about 2 percent of total value added, or USD 250 million, to Palestinian GDP.[24] The industry is by far the largest Palestinian exporter, accounting for about 17 percent of the total value of exported goods (figure 2.6).[25] Exports are based on significant endowments of the internationally renowned "Jerusalem Gold Stone," and on production know-how that has evolved over a long period.

The stone industry faces restrictions which impede its development and growth. These include "dual-list" prohibitions on the import of some production machinery, the complex and costly requirements required for export, and the general political and security environment that inhibits large capital investment of the

Figure 2.6 While Stone and Mineral Exports Have Increased in Nominal Terms, Their Share in Total Exports Dropped Despite a Meager Overall Export Growth

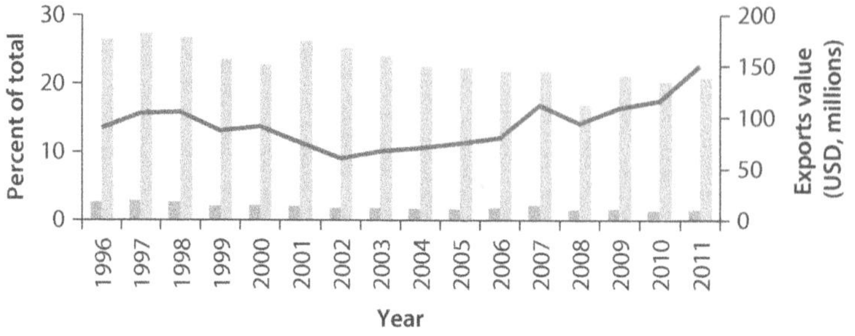

Source: Palestinian Central Bureau of Statistics (PCBS) and World Bank staff calculations.
Note: GDP = gross domestic product.

type needed in this industry. Area C is particularly affected. According to the Union of Stone and Marble Producers in the West Bank, no new permits have been issued to Palestinian companies to open quarries in Area C since 1994, even though the Oslo Accords provided for this.[26] Moreover, many previous permits have expired. Consequently, only a very small number of quarries are still operating legally in Area C.[27] These restrictions represent a major hurdle to the growth of an industry with substantial stone endowments in Area C—estimated at some 20,000 dunums of quarryable land and a potential endowment worth some USD 30 billion (or roughly three times annual Palestinian GDP).[28]

Unable to obtain permits, some companies continue operating—but these operations are often interrupted and result in substantial and unpredictable costs. According to the Union of Stone and Marble Producers, quarry closures have been accompanied by equipment confiscation and fines. Evidence collected from several companies reveals penalties ranging from 40,000 to 120,000 New Israeli Shekels. These closures also affect businesses downstream in the chain of production.[29] The Palestinian Union of Stone & Marble Industry cited some specific cases, where the inability to obtain permits has created a great deal of uncertainty and led to temporary closures of some quarries.[30]

In addition to the quarrying and processing of stone and marble, the growth potential of the smaller stone crushing industry is constrained. The stone crushing industry produces stone aggregates (mainly gravel) for the production of concrete, asphalt, and the subsurface layers of roads. Palestinian companies operating in this sector in the West Bank generate some USD 60 million in sales per year. An expansion of the industry would require tapping into stone deposits in Area C, given that the larger crushing quarries in the Qalandia area are nearing the end of their life cycle. No such permits appear to have been issued in the past 20 years.[31] On the other hand, the economic potential of this industry is demonstrated by the Israeli companies operating in Area C. These companies operate a number of crushers to produce construction stone and gravel in Area C. Official Israeli government estimates show that Israeli companies produce about 12 million tons of construction material, mainly gravel from these quarries.[32] Total market value of this production has been estimated at as much as USD 900 million (USD 756 million for construction stone and USD 144 million for gravel) in a 2011 report published jointly by the Ministry of National Economy of the Palestinian Authority and the Institute for Applied Research-Jerusalem (ARIJ).[33]

Potential in Marble and Stone Industries

The opportunity cost of restricted Palestinian access to and use marble and stone in Area C is significant. Accurate and comprehensive data are however unavailable—it would require access to a geological survey that includes Area C.[34] It would also require an assessment of the environmental impact of new quarries and plans that ensure that the industry expands in an environmentally sustainable manner. A conservative estimate of potential value added of USD 241 million per year can be made, though equivalent to 2 percent of 2011 GDP (see appendix A for the methodological details). This estimate excludes the stone aggregate potential in Area C.[35]

Construction and Real Estate

Restrictions on Access and Development

The growth of the Palestinian construction sector in the West Bank is severely constrained by Area C zoning rules. As mentioned in chapter 1, only a small part of Area C has not been reserved by Israel for other uses, such as Israeli settlements, closed military zones and nature reserves.[36] The impact of this zoning is to limit the land available for construction in the West Bank largely to Areas A and B, and this exerts strong upward pressure on the price of construction land, buildings, and physical infrastructure. OCHA (2009) estimates that in practice the Israeli Civil Administration allows Palestinians to construct freely in less than 1 percent of Area C—much of which is already built up.[37]

In the parts of Area C theoretically available to Palestinians for construction, it is almost impossible nowadays for Palestinians to obtain a construction permit, further limiting the supply of potential construction land. There is evidence to suggest that permit requirements are almost impossible to comply with, as demonstrated by a very low approval rate shown in table 2.1. Contributing factors include a lack of detailed plans for Palestinian villages, the Israeli Civil Administration's restrictive interpretation of the plans that do exist, and problems associated with proving ownership of the land.[38] Most Palestinian permit applications are rejected on the grounds that they are inconsistent with existing plans.[39] It was not always thus: Until the end of the 1970s, more than 90 percent of applications for building permits in rural areas (roughly equivalent to today's Area C) were granted. The approval percentage has since deteriorated, with the exception of two "blip" years in 2006 and 2008—as table 2.1 indicates.

Table 2.1 Palestinian Permits in Rural Areas and in Area C

	Applications for permits	Applications approved	Share of approved (%)
1972	2,199	2,134	97.0
1973	1,466	1,409	96.1
1988	1,682	532	31.6
1989	1,586	402	25.3
2000	182	5	2.7
2001	167	6	3.6
2002	159	6	3.8
2003	337	3	0.9
2004	250	5	2.0
2005	189	13	6.9
2006	176	43	24.4
2007	314	19	6.1
2008	336	74	22.0
2009	332	6	1.8
2010	444	7	1.6

Source: Bimkom (2008) and information provided by Bimkom on the basis of ICA data.

Notes: The figures for 1972 and 1973 only include construction for housing; additional permits were given for public buildings. The figures for 1972 and 1989 refer to the entire rural sector of the West Bank (but not the Palestinian cities), whereas the figures from 2000 and on refer only to Area C. Figures from 2000 onwards refer to "permits approved in principle" rather than actually approved. The ICA approves building in principle as long as the application satisfies a set of comprehensive prerequisites, but the permit is only issued after fees are paid and documents are brought in to be checked.

Such restrictions apply to all forms of Palestinian construction. These include public economic infrastructure (for example, roads, water reservoirs, waste treatment plants) and industrial plant. Area C restrictions also impact development in Areas A and B—since residential or commercial projects often require connections to existing service infrastructure (transport, water, energy) that needs to cross land in Area C. Rawabi, a new USD 1 billion residential and commercial town north-east of Ramallah, is a case in point (see box 2.2). Although 95 percent of the development is in Area A, the main access road runs through Area C, as do the waterlines. Delays in approving their construction are threatening to cause inception delays and could compromise the project's viability. A comparable situation has arisen in relation to the Jericho Industrial Park. Although Israel has welcomed its development, and although the park's internal infrastructure has been completed, the optimal access road to the park crosses Area C and has not yet been approved.

Area C restrictions are interrupting Palestinian settlements' natural growth. Many cities, towns, and villages have hit their expansion limits within Areas A and B and are in need of extra land on which to build. As figure 2.7 shows, the rate of growth in housing units in the West Bank has slowed markedly since 1995. While factors such as the disruptions of the second intifada may have contributed, the decline is consistent with the drop in the number of construction permits granted to Palestinians in Area C.

Box 2.2 Fighting the Current Restrictions to Develop a New City

With investments estimated close to USD 1 billion, Rawabi is the largest real estate investment ever made in Palestinian territories (funded by the Qatari company Diar and the Palestinian company Massar International). The project involves the creation of a new planned city north-west of Ramallah, initially composed of 6,000 residential units, along with various commercial units grouped around a commercial center, an industrial park, public spaces, as well as the necessary infrastructure. The city should accommodate around 25,000 residents by 2018 and aims to fulfil some of the unmet demand for housing mainly in Ramallah and Nablus. The project started in 2008, and it now employs around 4,500 people (between direct and indirect employees), working with 32 separate contractors.

The main advantage of the plot of land over which Rawabi is being developed is that it is almost entirely in Area A (95 percent), which is where the city is built. However, the development of the city has been facing a number of constraints related to Area C, which may cause a further delay in the delivery of the first 750 units, which are planned for the first quarter of 2014. The first constraint related to Area C concerns the main access road to the south of the city, which runs for 3.8 kilometers through Area C. This road is key to the viability of the project and the investors along with the Palestinian Authority (PA) and the international community have spent much political capital to obtain a temporary permit from the ICA, which has to be renewed every year. The temporariness of the permit creates uncertainty over the future of the city, as Rawabi would become an entirely unviable project should the permit not be renewed. In addition, the permit allows Rawabi to use a relatively narrow access road whose rehabilitation was delayed by one year due to lack of permit. This road is inadequate to accommodate the expected traffic flow of the city; therefore, the investors plan to build a parallel larger regional road, but the application filed three years ago has yet to receive an answer from the ICA. Rawabi would need an access road to the north as well (towards Nablus), but again the ICA has not yet approved the request for a 300 meter section in Area C connecting Rawabi to the existing main road to Nablus.

The access road is not the only constraint related to Area C that is challenging the development of Rawabi. Other utility services are also affected, including water and wastewater treatment. The water connection is stifled by the fact that a part of the 9 kilometer stretch connecting Rawabi to the existing piped system (in the village of Aboud) lies in Area C. Rawabi applied for a permit through the Joint Water Committee over four years ago but has not yet received a reply. Also, the most efficient solution for the wastewater treatment for the city would be a regional wastewater treatment servicing 18 villages around the area. This plant would allow the exploitation of economies of scale, which are key for this type of utility. However the site where the plant should be located is in Area C, which would require permit from the ICA.

The project would also involve the development of a logistics park in the outskirts of the city. However this park should be located between Areas B and C, thus again needing the Israeli authorities' approval. In addition to all of these constraints, it remains to be seen to what extent difficulties pertaining to law enforcement in Area C, which surrounds the city, may affect the appeal of a project like Rawabi.

Source: Interviews with representatives of Rawabi.

Figure 2.7 Growth in Housing Construction in the West Bank, 1967–2007

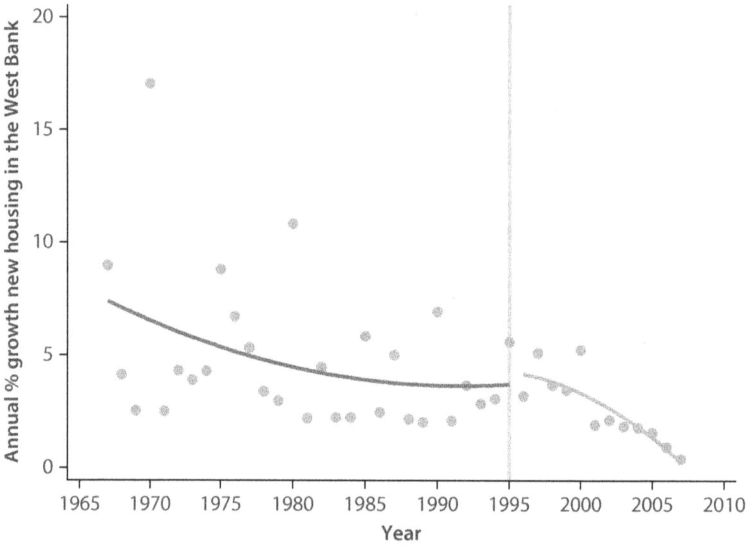

Source: PCBS 2009.

The difficulties of constructing in Area C have cramped the growth of the Palestinian cities of the West Bank, and have depressed construction demand. All West Bank cities' ability to expand is constrained in at least one direction by Area C, as table 2.2 shows—with cities like Qalqiliya and Tulkarm surrounded on all sides by Area C (and by the West Bank Separation Barrier). The table compares the degree of restrictiveness (number of sides on which expansion is blocked)[40] with the projected rate of population

Table 2.2 Estimated Population Growth and Area C Restrictiveness in the West Bank Governorates

	Pop 2007	Pop 2016	Δ% 07–16	Δ 07–16	Restrictiveness degree[a]
Bethlehem	122,086	155,607	27	33,521	3.5
Hebron	464,102	622,220	34	158,118	3
Jenin	149,377	187,905	26	38,528	1
Jericho	22,177	28,434	28	6,257	2.5
Nablus	175,195	214,903	23	39,708	3
Qalqiliya	54,908	69,198	26	14,290	4
Ramallah and Al-Bireh	143,169	185,701	30	42,532	3.5
Salfit	21,383	26,225	23	4,842	1.5
Tubas	32,982	44,555	35	11,573	1
Tulkarm	105,229	124,551	18	19,322	4

Source: PCBS 2008 and World Bank data.

a. Indicates the number of sides (out of 4) where the expansion of the urban area is blocked by the Area C border.

growth.[41] The governorates with the largest expected population growth (Hebron, Ramallah-Al-Bireh, Bethlehem, and Nablus) are all seriously cramped. As a result, most urban expansion has to be accommodated through vertical (rather than horizontal) building, which complicates the provision of urban services and may increase construction costs, as for instance water needs to be pumped, vertical transportation systems and earthquake proofing costs go up, and construction process requires more costly equipment.

Even more than in the larger cities, Israeli restrictions impair construction in the Palestinian communities located entirely or partially in Area C. Some 180,000 Palestinians live in Area C.[42] Only some 10 percent of the 130 or so Palestinian villages in Area C have Special Partial Outline Plans prepared by the Israeli Civil Administration (ICA). These act as master plans permitting the expansion of the community[43]—but strictly demarcate boundaries beyond which expansion cannot occur. The majority of villages have no such plans and are for the most part located on land classified as either agricultural or nature reserve land. Anecdotal evidence collected through interviews suggests that infrastructure projects serving the day-to-day needs of the Palestinians in Area C, such as the repair of roads or connections to water supply, are frequently delayed or denied by the ICA. Bedouin communities in Area C have been particularly disrupted by planning and zoning restrictions, and have experienced the demolition of even temporary structures. Although data are inadequate to estimate what construction activity might have taken place in Area C's Palestinian communities absent the restrictions, recent work by the International Peace and Cooperation Centre (IPCC) confirms that it is likely to have been substantial. The IPCC has, in some cases with the de facto approval of the ICA, begun developing plans to expand the built-up area of some communities in Area C.[44] This has helped secure existing structures against the risk of demolition and is allowing for the expansion of built-up areas.[45] Even though ICA approval is not official, where given, it has stimulated a flurry of construction activities. In Fasayil il Foqa, for instance, 30–40 percent of the tents in which residents had lived for years were replaced by concrete buildings within a few months.

Land and House Price Inflation
The restricted supply of construction land and inability to build in the vast majority of Area C has increased the price of West Bank land. Systematic land price data by areas are not available, but examples can show the magnitude of the price effect of these restrictions. In Khirbet Ilbadd in Ramallah for example, equivalent parcels of land in Areas B and C command very different prices: One dunum in Area B is evaluated at USD 250,000 versus one dunum in Area C evaluated at USD 80,000 only. Such price differentials are comparable to those reported by the World Bank (2008) as being driven purely by Area A/B/C classifications. The differentials reflect both the difficulty of developing Area C,[46] and the artificial inflation of land prices in Areas A and B. The cost of housing

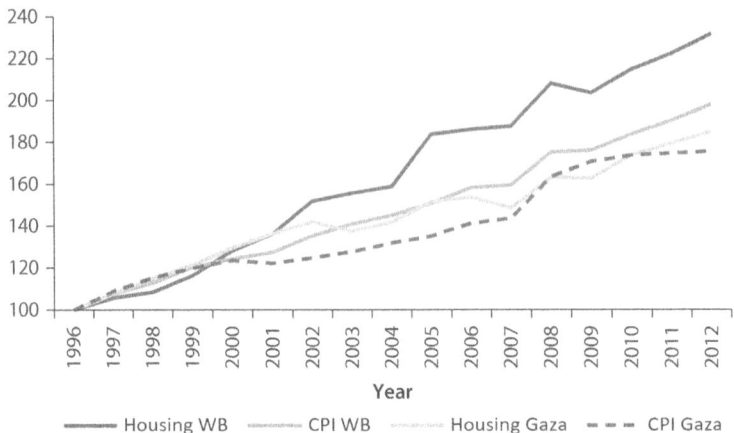

Figure 2.8 Housing Prices and Palestinian CPI, 1996–2012 (1996=100)

Source: PCBS.
Note: CPI = Consumer Price Index; WB = World Bank.

is similarly affected. Figure 2.8 shows that since 1996 housing prices in the West Bank have grown much more rapidly than the West Bank consumer price index—and faster than house prices in Gaza, which have tracked the consumer price index (CPI) more closely. A simple back of the envelope calculation based on these price differences suggests that the restrictions may have caused an increase in housing prices of around 24 percent.[47]

Construction Potential

By estimating the extent by which the potential quantity of housing has been reduced by the 24 percent price increase, we can conclude that the potential value added in the construction sector could be increased by as much as USD 239 million, or 2 percent of Palestinian GDP in 2011—if Palestinian companies are given easy access to construction land in Area C. Consumers would also benefit from lower average prices for housing, being able to acquire better housing and/or to consume other foregone goods and services. This estimate only accounts for residential and commercial construction, although other public infrastructure would clearly expand as well.[48] Please see appendix A for methodological details.

Tourism and the Dead Sea

Tourism currently makes a meager contribution to the Palestinian economy. It contributes less than 3 percent to Palestinian GDP and some 2 percent of total employment.[49] Following a sharp decline during the second intifada years, the Palestinian tourism industry has recovered and capacity has been expanded, with employment doubling (figure 2.9). The past three years have seen an average of more than 500,000 arrivals, with total stays of more than 1.2 million room nights per year,[50] up from well below 50,000 arrivals in 2000–02 (figure 2.10).

Area C—Output Potential of Key Sectors of the Palestinian Economy

Figure 2.9 Following the Second Intifada, the Employment in the Hotel and Restaurants Sector (A Good Proxy for Tourism) Doubled

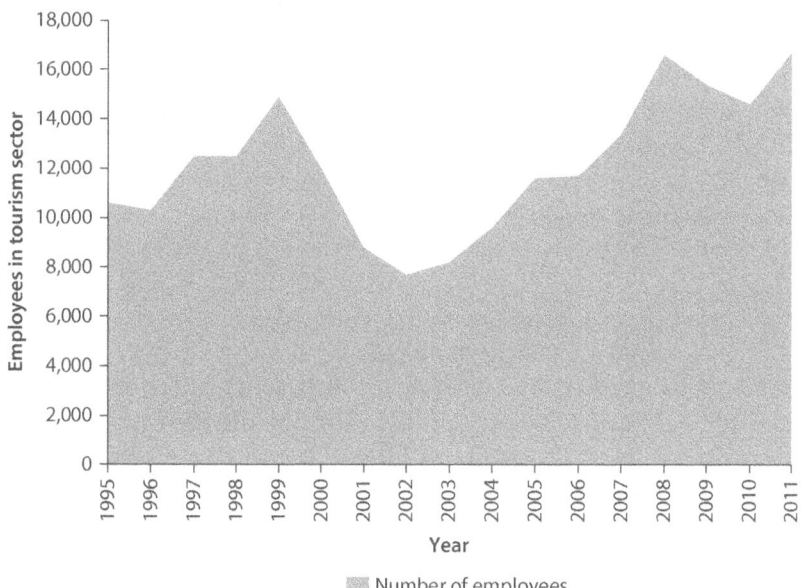

Source: World Bank and United Nations World Tourism Organization (UNWTO).

Figure 2.10 Following the Second Intifada, the Number of Hotels Increased Only Modestly, but Hotel Activity Increased Dramatically

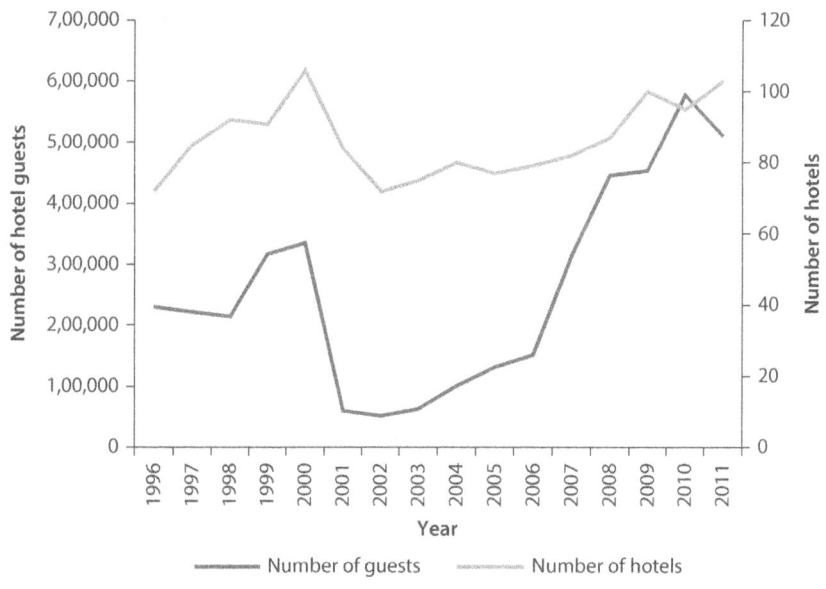

Source: World Bank and United Nations World Tourism Organization (UNWTO).

The Palestinian territories are home to some of the greatest tourist attractions in the world. The Dead Sea and its surrounding landscape, the Mediterranean Sea coast in Gaza, and a plethora of religious and historical sites represent a world-class tourism endowment. Some of the most significant religious sites in the world for Muslims, Christians, and Jews are to be found in the Palestinian territories. The PA has submitted 20 sites to United Nations Educational Scientific and Cultural Organization (UNESCO) for consideration as World Cultural Heritage locations, and while Bethlehem was so recognized by UNESCO in 2012 more recognitions are likely in the future. The Palestinian territories thus have the potential to attract large additional numbers of tourists, as figure 2.11 suggests.

The development of the Palestinian tourism potential is hindered by a number of factors. They include the fragile political and security situation, and the various restrictions imposed by Government of Israel (GoI) on movement, access, and physical development. Gaza and its Mediterranean coast, for instance, are in practice inaccessible to foreign tourists for several reasons. Perceived or real security issues in the West Bank undoubtedly discourage potential tourists. Furthermore, the development of tourism requires both private and public investments, and these are constrained by the same factors that affect Palestinian development activities elsewhere. The limitations on economic activity in Area C, however, are of particular importance because even if all the other significant constraints are removed, inability to develop tourism capacity in Area C would substantially limit the growth potential of this sector.

Area C and the Dead Sea

Area C has large tourism growth potential. Area C, excluding Jerusalem, is home to around 3,110 archeological sites registered by the Palestinian Ministry of Tourism and Antiquities—of which 443 are in the Seam Zone,[51] and 247 in

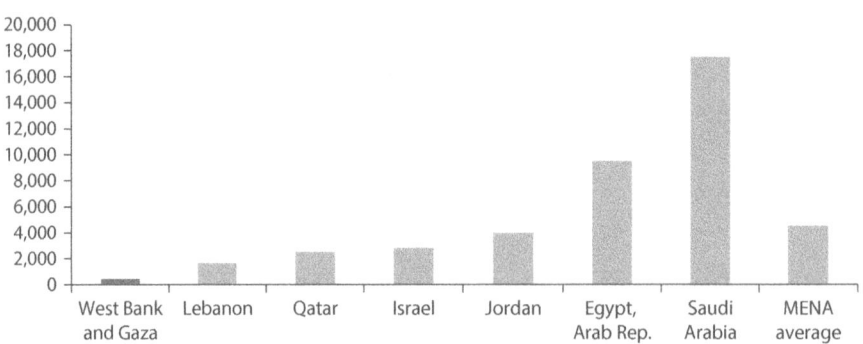

Figure 2.11 Number of International Tourist Arrivals in the Palestinian Territories (1000)

Source: World Bank and United Nations World Tourism Organization (UNWTO).
Note: MENA = Middle East and North Africa.

various settlements' municipal areas. Among the most significant Area C sites are Sabastiya, Qumran, and Herodion (the latter two are currently managed by the Israeli Nature and Parks Authority). Many currently "forgotten" archeological sites could become important tourist destinations in the future, and feature in UNESCO's "Inventory of Cultural and Natural Heritage Sites of Potential Outstanding Universal Value in Palestine."

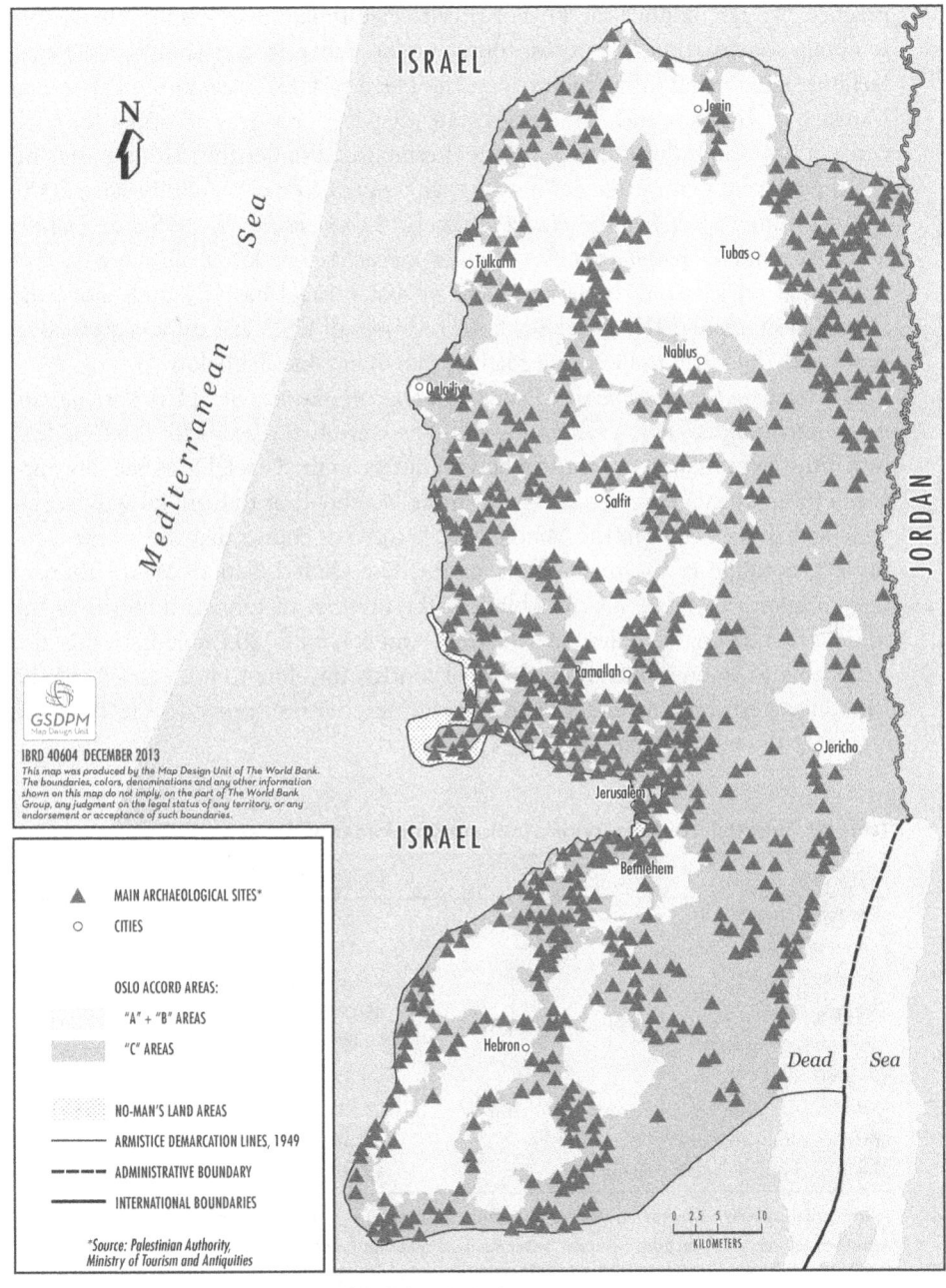

Source: Ministry of Tourism and Antiquities of the Palestinian Authority.

The legal basis for Palestinians to develop Dead Sea tourism is in place—but this has not been translated into reality. Annex VI, Article V of the Interim Agreement includes specific mention of tourism around the Dead Sea, stating that "…the two sides shall examine ways to ….(5) encourage joint ventures in the tourism field in all areas of mutual benefit including on the Dead Sea. In this regard, Palestinian private projects as well as joint ventures in accordance with the Declaration of Principles (DOP) will be located as agreed on the shore of the Dead Sea."[52] In practice, though, neither the PA nor private Palestinian investors have been able to obtain construction permits for tourism-related investments (hotels, recreation facilities, supporting infrastructure) on the Dead Sea. Officials in the Palestinian Ministry of Tourism and Antiquities state that the only way to apply for such permits is through the Joint Committees established under the Oslo Agreement, but the relevant committee has not met with any degree of regularity since 2000.

On the other hand, both Israel and Jordan have developed the Dead Sea as a tourist destination and are reaping significant economic benefits. The Jordanian shore has five hotels that are classified as either 5-star or 4-star. Israel has 15 hotels along the Dead Sea shore. In 2012, Dead Sea hotel revenues of USD 291 million accrued to Israel, and USD 128 million to Jordan, as shown in table 2.3 below.

It is reasonable to assume that Palestinian tourism investors would, in the long run, not directly compete with Israel for tourists. There are two reasons for this. The first is that the great majority of those who visit hotels on the Israeli Dead Sea shore are Israeli (83 percent). The second is the strong likelihood of tourism growth worldwide and, in particular in the Middle East, granted of course that the recent security deterioration in the region is overcome. The United Nations World Tourism Organization projects a near doubling in the number of tourists destined to the Middle East, from 36 million in 2010 to 69 million by 2020 (table 2.4). It is also reasonable to assume that the number of tourists traveling to both Israel and the Palestinian territories would increase significantly with improved security in the region, to the mutual benefit of both parties.

Table 2.3 Selected Dead Sea Tourism Indicators for Jordan and Israel

Dead Sea	Jordan	Israel
Number of hotels	5	15
Room capacity	1,415	3,987
Number of guests	231,119	878,700
Bed bights	450,955	2,315,800
Occupancy rate (bed)	55	71
Average stay	1.95	2.64
Number of employees in tourist hotels	1,585	2,882
% of total tourism employment	3.68	2.8*
Dead sea hotel revenues (million USD)	127.54*	290.9

Source: Jordan data are taken from the Ministry of Tourism and Antiquities' Tourism Statistical Newsletter

Note: Data on Israel are taken from the Israeli Center Bureau of Statistics' Time Series DataBank. Value-added data are taken from the Tourism Satellite Accounts for both countries.

a. World Bank Staff calculations based on mentioned sources.

Area C—Output Potential of Key Sectors of the Palestinian Economy

Table 2.4 The Number of Tourists Has Been Growing Around the World and Is Expected to Continue with Strong Growth by 2020 Worldwide and in the Middle East

	Number of tourists			Market share		Average annual growth rate
	Million					Percent
	1995	2010	2020	1995	2020	1995–2020
World	565	1,006	1,561	100	100	4.1
Africa	20	47	77	3.6	5	5.5
United States	110	190	282	19.3	18.1	3.8
East Asia and the Pacific	81	195	397	14.4	25.4	6.5
Europe	336	527	717	59.8	45.9	3.1
Middle East	14	36	69	2.2	4.4	6.7
South Asia	4	11	19	0.7	1.2	6.2

Source: United Nations World Trade Organization, http://www.unwto.org/facts/eng/vision.htm.

Value Added to Tourism

Israel can serve as a useful proxy to gauge the potential of Palestinian Dead Sea tourism investments. Most Israeli hotels and resorts on the Dead Sea are on a 6 kilometer stretch of the southern shore. Based on the 1967 borders, the Palestinian Dead Sea Coast is about 40 kilometers long. While not all of this is suitable for resort development, a conservative assumption is that at least 6 kilometers could be developed into resorts similar to those in Israel and Jordan. It is not unreasonable to assume that Palestinian room capacity could amount at 4,000 units, equivalent to the current room capacity on the Israeli Dead Sea shore. Without discounting other important factors—security, movement, the need for branding and marketing—over time the Palestinians could be expected to develop a Dead Sea hotel industry of comparable profitability to Israel. This would provide annual revenues of some USD 290 million and value added of about USD126 million, equivalent to 1 percent of 2011 Palestinian GDP (see appendix A for details on the calculation methodology). Assuming labor productivity equivalent to that in the Israeli tourism industry, direct employment of about 2,900 workers could be created.

The opportunity cost of the restrictions on the tourism industry, however, is not limited to the Dead Sea alone. As discussed above, the Dead Sea is only one potential tourism destination in Area C. Unfortunately, sufficient data are not available to carry out a similar calculation of the opportunity cost associated with the restrictions that prevent the development of tourist destinations in other parts of Area C. That opportunity cost is not negligible, however, and is best demonstrated by the tourism activity, which has already been developed by Israel in some parts of Area C. Namely, Israel has been generating revenues from historical and nature tourism sites in the Dead Sea area and around Jericho since 1976.[53] The five main tourist archeological sites in Area C that generate revenue for Israel are Qumran, Ein Fashkha, Herodion, Ein Fara in Wadi Qelt, and the Good

Table 2.5 Revenues Collected from West Bank Sites Managed and Operated by the Israeli Nature and Parks Authority

Site	Number of visitors	Estimated revenues (USD million)
Qumran	373,826	2.05
Ein Fashkha	101,693	0.56
Herodion	86,375	0.47
Ein Fara	133,123	0.73
Good Samaritan	39,131	0.16

Source: Israeli Nature and Parks Authority.

Samaritan. In 2011, Qumran National Park, the site of the Dead Sea Scrolls, was the fifth most visited pay-per-view site with 373,826 visitors.[54] This generates estimated revenues of USD 2.05 million in entry fees alone.[55] Ein Fashkha, a nature reserve which had 101,639 visitors in 2011, generated an estimated USD 0.56 million (see table 2.5 for details). The table below shows the sites, the number of visitors in 2011, and the estimated revenues generated in that year. In addition to destinations in Area C currently run by Israel, there is a large number of other sites of important historical significance that Palestinians could develop into attractive tourism destinations.

Telecommunications

The development of Palestinian mobile and landline services in the West Bank is significantly constrained by poor access to Area C, the difficulty of obtaining permits to build infrastructure, restrictions on use of the electromagnetic spectrum and problems with importing essential telecommunications equipment, including fiber optics, switches, and Ethernet materials. The telecommunications sector contributed 5.6 percent to Palestinian GDP in 2011, in line with countries at similar levels of development—but the sector has not been able to meet demand or attain achievable price and quality standards. This is in large part due to the need, as specified in the Oslo Agreements, for various Israeli permissions.[56] The agreements leave important regulatory decisions to a Joint Technical Committee; the JTC, however, has not been convening as often as required and the outcomes of its meetings have been unsatisfactory from a Palestinian perspective. The JTC last met in June 2012 after a break of more than a year and a half.

Access and Permits
The Mobile Operators—Jawwal and Wataniya
Restrictions on building cellular infrastructure in Area C limit Palestinian mobile operators' ability to serve Palestinian residents in this area and also in large swathes in Areas A and B that would need to be connected through infrastructure in Area C. This is manifest in the overall cellular penetration rate in the Palestinian territories; While Internet and landline penetration rates are comparable to other nearby Arab countries, cellular penetration is only 77 percent—much lower than

the Middle East and North Africa average of 123 percent. Some communities in Areas A and B cannot obtain Palestinian cellular service at all; this problem is more acute in Area C, where the mobile penetration rate is a mere 16 percent. The inability to serve customers in Area C and in some parts of Areas A and B lead to potential revenue losses for the operators.

To provide optimal signal coverage throughout the West Bank, the two Palestinian mobile operators would need to erect a total of 330 towers in Area C. Over the last 10 years, one operator has applied for licenses from the Israeli Authorities to erect 60 such towers. So far, only one final approval for a single site has been granted. The process to apply for a license to build infrastructure has been described by the Palestinian mobile operators as extremely ambiguous and time consuming. One carrier reports having been told that the GoI would provide permits to build towers in Area C but only to an Israeli firm. In this case, the Palestinian carrier would have to sign a contract to build and maintain towers with an Israeli firm, instead of the company that already builds its infrastructure in the rest of the West Bank, substantially adding to costs. In addition, the Palestinian carrier would not be able to directly link the towers in Area C to its network in Areas A and B. Instead they would have to be linked through an Israeli network passing through Israel, and then through international switches to the carrier's network in the West Bank. This again would add substantial transmission costs.

Because Area C connects Areas A and B and includes many high points, it offers many of the best locations for towers. However, restrictions on building infrastructure in Area C force the Palestinian operators to lay a larger number of towers in suboptimal locations in Areas A and B to provide good coverage. One of the operators reports, that over the last 10 years, it has erected 150 towers that would not have been needed if they were able to construct in Area C. The consequent efficiency losses are estimated by the two operators at about USD 11.5 million per year. This is ultimately reflected in consumer prices, and one operator reports that its end prices are on average 15–16 percent higher compared to a situation where the company would be able to operate in Area C. The Palestinian carriers report that the lack of telecom infrastructure in Area C also increases the load on the already strained systems in Areas A and B resulting in dropped calls and lower quality of service. The high prices and low quality reduce the competitiveness of the Palestinian operators and encourage customers to use Israeli providers.

Box 2.3 Serving the Residents of Marah Rabah and Teqou in Area B

The village of Marah Rabah and the town of Teqou are both part of the Bethlehem governorate in central West Bank and lie within Area B. Marah Rabah has a population of over 1,320 while Teqou is home for 8,881 Palestinians.[a] To provide good mobile coverage for the residents of these two areas, the Palestinian operator had to erect three towers in suboptimal locations in Area B due to the inability to build infrastructure in Area C. In a

box continued next page

Box 2.3 Serving the Residents of Marah Rabah and Teqou in Area B *(continued)*

hypothetical situation where Area C restrictions are not applicable, the operator would be able to provide coverage to these two areas through placing a single tower in Area C.

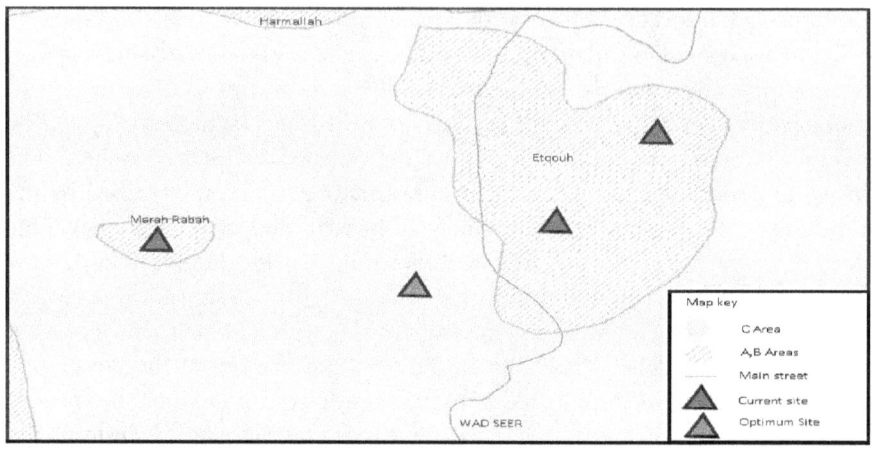

Source: Map provided by one of the Palestinian mobile operators.
a. PCBS population census, 2008.

The lack of coverage in Area C and some parts of Areas A and B obliges residents to rely on Israeli carriers or to roam on Israeli networks. It is estimated that some 150–200,000, or 5–7 percent, of mobile subscribers in the West Bank, obtain services through one of the Israeli providers. As the Israeli firms do not pay taxes to the PA, this also leads to losses in public revenues. Customers using Palestinian phones in areas that are not covered by Palestinian carriers must pay large roaming fees to Israeli firms, who cover almost all of the West Bank in providing service to the Israeli settlements.

The Landline Operator—Paltel

Permit problems have made it difficult for Paltel to expand its customer base in Area C, and to upgrade services to certain places in Areas A and B. Paltel reports that almost 40 percent of its Area C permit requests are rejected. The company currently provides landline and asymmetric digital subscriber line (ADSL) services to only 8,000 out of the 16,300 households that comprise the Area C market. The majority of the remaining households rely on Israeli operators. Due to permit problems, the company finds it extremely difficult to upgrade services in many places in the West Bank that are connected through fiber-optic cables running through Area C. Time required to get a permission to operate in these areas can be up to 12 times higher than the normal rate. This has restrained the company's ability to upgrade its quality of service in many places in the West Bank including areas in Jenin, Tulkarm, Qalqilya, and Bethlehem. This leads to high churn rates

Area C—Output Potential of Key Sectors of the Palestinian Economy

among customers who are dissatisfied with the service quality, some of which shift to Israeli providers.

The inability to develop infrastructure in Area C is also associated with higher costs for serving customers in Areas A and B. Area C's strategic location as the land that connects Areas A and B makes it ideal to place central fiber lines that can link customers from all three areas to the system. However, due to restrictions on building infrastructure there, the company is forced to lay down its fiber network through longer detours bypassing Area C, which significantly increases the cost. These longer fiber networks also require higher maintenance costs.

Box 2.4 Suboptimal Transmission Paths

The city of Qalqilya is one of the major Palestinian cities in Northern West bank. It serves as a center for the Qalqilya governorate and it houses around 41,739[a] Palestinians. To serve the residents of Qalqilya, the city had to be connected through a fiber transmission network in the city of Azun to the East. The most optimal route to establish a transmission path from Azun to Qalqilya would have been through a 9 kilometer road in Area C that extends in a straight line from the East to the West. The company, however, was not granted a license by the GoI to dig this path. It, therefore, had to roll out fiber from Azun through various villages in Area B including Kafr Thulth, Ras 'Atiye, Habla to Qalqilya in order to limit its presence in Area C, and hence reduce the number of required approvals. This suboptimal transmission path extended over 15 kilometers and increased the cost of this operation by more than 60 percent.

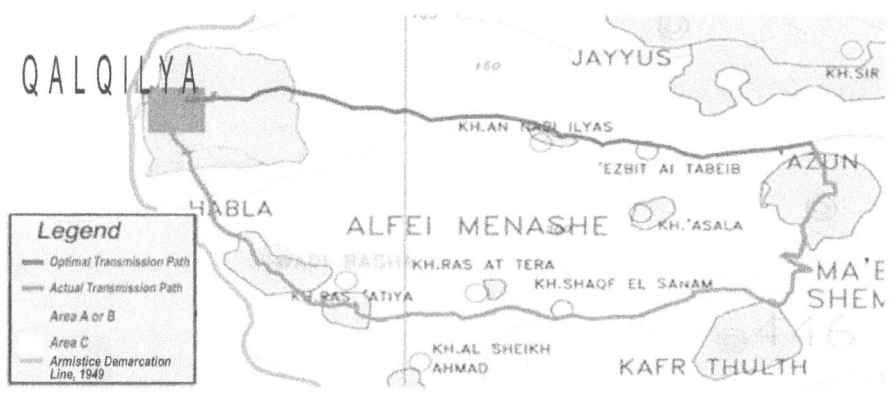

Source: Map provided by the Palestinian landline operator.
a. PCBS population census, 2008.

As a result of the PA's inability to provide security in Area C, Paltel's Area C network segments suffer from frequent theft that targets valuable copper wiring. It is estimated that the theft incidents cost the company around USD 340,000 per year mainly due to the cost of additional fiber and copper needed to relink the damaged network segments. In order to try and protect its network in Area C, the company applies additional security measures, which also raise its cost.

Paltel also faces high competition by Israeli telecommunications firms in the Palestinian market. These firms use infrastructure laid in Area C to serve Israeli settlements as points of presence to sell Internet services in the West Bank to wholesale providers as well as individual households. This competition is estimated to lead to foregone potential revenue that is estimated by the operator to be about USD 4.5 million per year.

Frequencies

The Israeli Authorities have so far only released limited 2G frequencies to the two Palestinian mobile operators (18 percent of the 900 megahertz band and 4 percent of the 1,800 megahertz band). The two Palestinian operators serve more than 3 million subscribers with these limited frequencies, resulting in loads higher than specified by international standards and obliging them to build multiple towers close to one another to reduce congestion and maintain adequate service.

Israel's failure to provide Palestinian carriers frequencies for 3G service represents a major competitive disadvantage and a threat to the future viability of the industry. Palestinian mobile operators do not have any access to the 2,100 megahertz band through which they would provide 3G services, and are unable to offer mobile broadband or high-speed data services to their customers. Notably, the demand for such services among Palestinian customers has been on the rise as the number of smart phone users in the Palestinian territories grew from 3 percent in 2010 to 17 percent over the last two years, even though they currently cannot access full features of the phone nor use mobile broadband. One of the Palestinian operators reports that some customers in this fast-growing category of users have already shifted towards Israeli firms to get 3G services. The operator also reports that Israeli companies are aware of this potential market and have recently been marketing 3G to West Bankers. If Israel does allow Palestinian access to the 2,100 megahertz band, Palestinian carriers will have to make sizable new investments in infrastructure—which again raises the issue of access to Area C. Area C offers ideal sites for 3G infrastructure that can simultaneously serve customers in Areas A, B, and C. Without such access, it would be extremely difficult for Palestinian carriers to compete with Israeli firms. The Palestinian mobile companies believe that as the number of smart phone users increases and the world moves on to 4G services, their very survival may depend upon being able to access 3G frequencies.

Telecommunications Potential

The benefits of addressing the current restrictions would be significant. Annual potential revenues lost have been conservatively estimated at some USD 21 million, with annual additional costs incurred total c. USD 27 million. Based on these figures, the foregone (and thus potential) value added to the sector is estimated to be USD 48 million. This represents some 0.5 percent of 2011 Palestinian GDP. Please see appendix A for methodological details.

Cosmetics

The economic potential offered by the Dead Sea includes cosmetics. Taking advantage of the therapeutic qualities of some Dead Sea minerals, both Israel and Jordan have developed sizeable cosmetics industries. Quantifying the benefits that can be ascribed to Dead Sea minerals is not easy,[57] but we know that some 50 companies in Israel produce cosmetic products relying primarily on Dead Sea salts and minerals. The largest one of them, Ahava, exports to about 30 countries and generates annual revenues of about USD 150 million.[58] According to the Israel Trade Commission, the total exports of the Israeli cosmetics industry amounts to USD 165 million per year.[59] The counterpart industry is much smaller on the Jordanian side with some estimates putting total annual sales at USD 30 million.[60] Success in the cosmetics industry depends in particular on marketing and branding, at which Ahava excels. Ahava's example illustrates the potential that exists for entrepreneurial Palestinian businesses with access to the base materials. Several factors could work to the advantage of potential Palestinian entrants into the global cosmetics market. First, the global demand for natural cosmetics products is expanding sharply and is expected to rise from USD 7.6 billion in 2012 to USD 13.2 billion in 2018.[61] Second, barriers to entry in the cosmetics industry are not large—it is an industry characterized by monopolistic competition. Third is the availability of cheap and unique raw materials. Fourth, the industry would benefit from the know-how accumulated by successful Palestinian pharmaceutical manufacturers. Last but not least, there is scope for cooperation with the Israeli cosmetics industry; Israeli companies appear to be interested in working with Palestinian companies to help them gain access to lucrative Arab and other predominantly Muslim markets.[62]

Notes

1. See, for example, Berdegue, J. A., E. Ramirez, T. Reardon, and G. Escobar, 2001. "Rural Nonfarm Employment and Incomes in Chile," and Lanjouw, P., and A. Shariff, 2002. "Rural Nonfarm Employment in India: Access, Income, and Poverty Impact." The World Bank Working Paper No. 81.
2. The median nominal daily wage (MNDW) in agriculture (which was lower than in the rest of the economy to start with) grew 20 percent more slowly than the MNDW in the economy as a whole between 1997 and 2011.
3. Land Research Center, 2010. "Land Suitability for Reclamation April 2010 and Development in the West Bank. Hebron, Palestine."
4. The World Bank, 2010. "The Underpinnings of the Future Palestinian State: Sustainable Growth and Institutions." The report notes that in 2010, while "the Israeli military removed some 80 roadblocks that impeded vehicular access for limited numbers of farmers to agricultural land in Area C, no improvement was observed regarding access to much larger agricultural areas."
5. Palestinian Water Authority, 2012. "National Water Strategy for Palestine, Ramallah."
6. World Bank, 2009. "Assessment of Restrictions on Palestinian Water Sector Development." Sector Note.

7. Selby, Jan, 2013. "Cooperation, Domination and Colonisation: The Israeli-Palestinian Joint Water Committee," *Water Alternatives* 6 (1): 1–24.
8. See Interim Agreement, Annex III, Article 40: 6.
9. PCBS (2009c), Water Statistics in the Palestinian Territory Annual Report, 2008, Ramallah, Palestine.
10. Selby, "Cooperation, Domination and Colonisation."
11. By 2007, the Palestinian population had access to only about one quarter of the ration of their Israeli counterparts: West Bank Palestinians consumed about 123 liters per capita per day while Israelis about 544 liters per day. See World Bank, 2009. "Assessment of Restrictions on Palestinian Water Sector Development." Sector Note.
12. Interviews with farmers in the Jordan Valley indicate that there are around 300 packing facilities for agricultural products in the Jordan Valley, of which only two are Palestinians, while the rest of the facilities belong to the settlements.
13. According to B'tselem, 2010, the Palestinian land which has remained west of the barrier and thus inaccessible to most residents of the West Bank amounts to 119,500 dunums.
14. Glover, S., and A. Hunter, 2010. "Meeting Future Palestinian Water Needs." Palestinian Policy Research Institute (MAS).
15. Assuming that only 15 percent of the rangelands in Area C are currently accessible to Palestinians—see Dudeen, B. A., 2002. "Land Degradation in Palestine: Main Factors, Present Status and Trends." Land Research Center, Hebron.
16. PCBS, 2009.
17. ICL Periodic Report for 2012, p. 12.
18. Staff estimates based on data from Israeli and Jordanian official statistics, annual reports of the Arab Potash Company PLC, Israeli Chemicals Ltd. (ICL), and data on the cosmetic industries in both countries.
19. Potash is the common name given to various potassium salts. It is an important plant nutrient and is used for fertilizer.
20. See ICL Periodic Report for 2012, p. 38. The ICL report and several other online sources show significantly higher current potash consumption and demand forecast than that shown by the Food and Agriculture Organization of the United Nations in its "Current World Fertilizer Trends and Outlook to 2016."
21. ICL Periodic Report for 2012, p. 59.
22. The data on bromine production in Jordan shown on the chart are significantly larger (by about 100,000 tons) than the production of the Jordan Bromine Company Limited, which is used to calculate bromine revenues in Jordan. The US Geological Survey, 2011, "Minerals Yearbook" also estimates bromine production in Jordan at 300,000 tons. It is thus possible that there are other producers of bromine in Jordan and that we have underestimated the revenues and value added generated by bromine production in Jordan.
23. ICL Periodic Report for 2012, p. 44.
24. The employment figure cited in the text is based on the still-unpublished survey of the stone and marble industry in the West Bank being prepared by United Nations Industrial Development Organization (UNIDO). The value-added figure is taken from official PCBS industry statistics for 2010 (ISIC Rev. 4, lines 810 and 2396). Another document, entitled "Stone & Marble in Palestine: Developing a Strategy for

the Future," published by the Union of Stone and Marble Industry in July 2011, included significantly higher estimates for the size of this industry and noted that it accounts for 5 percent of West Bank and Gaza GDP and employs 15,000–20,000 people. That report, however, is based on older data; official statistics show that the relative size of the sector in the economy has decreased in recent years.

25. Based on 2011 export data.
26. "The Israeli side shall consider any request by Palestinian entrepreneurs to operate quarries in Area C on its merits," The Israeli Palestinian Interim Agreement, Article 31, 4.
27. Union of Stone and Marble Industry, 2011, op. cit.
28. Ibid.
29. Ibid., p. 18 "Nowhere is the situation more acute than in Beit Fajjar, south of Bethlehem. There are approximately 40 quarries in 2,500 dunums of land, much of which is in Area C and unpermitted. Citing the lack of permission to operate, the activities at the quarries have been repeatedly interrupted by the IDF, which has seized numerous pieces of equipment and imposed fines for them to be returned. This pattern intensified during 2010, to the point that quarries have largely been rendered inoperable for the last several months. In turn, this had a direct knock on effect on the 150 factories and workshops in Beit Fajjar that are supplied by the quarries."
30. Union of Stone and Marble Industry, 2011. "Stone & Marble in Palestine: Developing a Strategy for the Future," p. 18; "Nowhere is the situation more acute than in Beit Fajjar, south of Bethlehem. There are approximately 40 quarries in 2,500 dunums of land, much of which is in Area C and unpermitted. Citing the lack of permission to operate, the activities at the quarries have been repeatedly interrupted by the Israeli Defence Forces (IDF), which has seized numerous pieces of equipment and imposed fines for them to be returned. This pattern intensified during 2010, to the point that quarries have largely been rendered inoperable for the last several months. In turn, this had a direct knock on effect on the 150 factories and workshops in Beit Fajjar that are supplied by the quarries."
31. Interviews with the Palestinian Authority and the private sector.
32. Yesh Din, 2009. "Petition for an Order Nisi and an Interim Injunction, The Supreme Court of Israel, Jerusalem," which quotes the "National Blueprint (NBP) 14b—NBP of Mining and Quarrying Sites for the Construction and Road Building Business" (2008).
33. As discussed above, it has been estimated that Israeli stone aggregates industry in Area C generates about $900 million per year.
34. This information was obtained from the Union of Stone and Marble Producers and in interviews with representatives of the Palestinian Authority. The Union reported that a geological survey has been conducted recently by the Palestinian Authority for Areas A and B, but that the Israeli authorities did not permit the survey to be extended to Area C.
35. Which could be considerable. Israeli companies operating in Area C produce some 12 million tons of construction material, most of which is gravel, according to official Israeli sources. The market value of this gravel production has been estimated by the Ministry of National Economy of the PA and the Institute for Applied Research—Jerusalem at USD 144 million.

36. This has been documented in previous World Bank reports and confirmed in interviews with the Palestinian Authority, Palestinian private sector and Bimkom (an Israeli nongovernmental organization [NGO]).
37. OCHA, 2009, op. cit.
38. Ibid.
39. Ibid. See also Bimkom, 2008. "The Prohibited Zone: Israeli Planning Policy in the Palestinian Villages in Area C."
40. For each of the four cardinal directions, the share of the city bordering Area C is evaluated. If this share is close to 100 percent, then the index uses a value of 1 for that direction; if it is close to 50 percent, it uses 0.5, and if it is close to zero, it uses zero.
41. East Jerusalem is not included because it is directly controlled by the Israeli authorities and is thus is not under the planning control of the Palestinian Authority.
42. The Palestinian population located in Area C is estimated by the Israeli planning organization Bimkom to be 180,000 (this includes those whose house is located in Area C but are part of communities which are split between Area C and Areas A or/and B); PCBS data shows that around 113,000 people live in communities entirely located in Area C.
43. World Bank, 2008. "The Economic Effects of Restricted Access to Land in the West Bank."
44. These are intended to replace the outdated "blue line" documents. Blue line documents are demarcations of community boundaries that do not include any infrastructure or roads.
45. IPCC, 2013. "Action Plan: Planning Intervention in Area C." Mimeo.
46. In recent years, a number of Palestinian real estate developers acquired land in Area C with the intention of developing relatively large residential projects there—but none of them have been able to start any such development yet. Amaar, the real estate development arm of the Palestine Investment Fund, acquired 150 dunums of land south-east of Jenin in Areas A and C to develop a complex of 3,000 residential units. The company realized that obtaining permits for a project situated partly in Area C was not feasible, and adjusted its plans to create a smaller residential project of 1,000 units located entirely in area A—with less investment and less employment generation and value added potential.
47. This calculation is performed along similar lines to the differences-in-differences estimation, that is, $\Delta price^H_{WB-G} = (\Delta price^H_{WB} - \Delta price^{All}_{WB}) - (\Delta price^H_{Gaza} - \Delta price^{All}_{Gaza})$, where $\Delta price All$ is the change in CPI between 1996 and 2012 for either West Bank or Gaza and $\Delta price H$ is the change in housing prices over the same period.
48. In the Palestinian National Accounts for 2011, total construction output was USD 902 million (PCBS, 2012d)—far exceeding expenditure on building construction of USD 518 million (PCBS, 2012c).
49. PCBS, 2012. "Tourism Activities Survey."
50. PCBS, 2012. "Hotel Activities in Palestine: Annual Bulletin."
51. "The Seam Zone" is the term used to refer to West Bank land located east of the Green Line and west of the Separation Barrier and is an area to which Palestinians are not normally granted access.

52. Article 4, paragraph 2 of the Declaration of Principles of September 3, 1993 states that the jurisdiction over tourism affairs would immediately be transferred to the Palestinian Authority: "Preparatory Transfer of Powers and Responsibilities: In the rest of the West Bank, five specific spheres—education and culture, health, social welfare, direct taxation, and tourism—are to be transferred to Palestinian representatives through early empowerment. Additional spheres may be transferred as agreed by the sides. The DOP proposed that this transfer of powers take place immediately following the implementation of the Gaza-Jericho Agreement."
53. B'tselem, 2011. "Dispossession and Exploitation. Israel's Policy in the Jordan Valley and the Northern Dead Sea."
54. Report of the Nature and Parks Authority (2012).
55. Revenue was calculated by multiplying the number of visitors by the average entry fee, so it is probably an underestimation since adults, who face the highest entry fee, are also usually the group that frequents these places more than others.
56. Oslo Agreement, Annex III, Protocol on Israeli-Palestinian Cooperation in Economic and Development Programs, and Interim Agreement, Annex III, Art. 36.
57. Because these industries (both in Israel and Jordan) consist of a relatively large number of privately owned companies and because not all of them (particularly in Israel) use Dead Sea minerals as primary inputs in their products.
58. CNN Money, 2009. "Turning Dead Sea Mud into Money."
59. http://www.israeltrade.org.au/spotlight-on-israels-cosmetics-industry/.
60. *Taipei Times*, "Jordan Eying a Big Share of Dead Sea Cosmetics Market." http://www.taipeitimes.com/News/bizfocus/archives/2010/03/21/2003468511.
61. The information is based on "Organic Personal Care Products Market for Skin Care, Hair Care, Oral Care and Cosmetics—Global Industry Analysis, Size, Share, Growth, Trends and Forecast, 2012–2018." http://www.cosmeticsandtoiletries.com/formulating/category/natural/Demand-for-Organic-Beauty-to-Grow-to-Over-13-Billion-by-2018-Report-Says-213160491.html.
62. The interest in cooperation was confirmed in meetings with representatives of the Israeli cosmetics industry.

CHAPTER 3

Indirect Benefits

In addition to the direct benefits discussed in chapter 2, the indirect benefits of removing the restrictions in Area C would be significant. Indirect costs and benefits can be divided into those related to physical and institutional infrastructure, and spillover-related costs and benefits. The first set is driven by the impact of Israeli restrictions on the *quality* and *cost* of infrastructure; the impact of the restrictions in this instance is difficult to measure, and no attempt to do so is made here. Nonetheless, the effects are considerable and are alluded to below. The second set of costs and benefits derive from the fact that sectors are linked, with one using the outputs of another as production inputs—and those have been quantified.

Secondary Costs and Benefits Related to Infrastructure

Israeli restrictions further fragment an already-small market. The development of cost-effective transport infrastructure is impossible in most of the West Bank, making it more difficult to achieve economies of scale and contain costs. Poor transport infrastructure also affects labor mobility, access to public services, and the quality of life in general. The West Bank's main urban and peri-urban centers in Areas A and B amount to islands surrounded by the sea of Area C, lack of access to which has stymied any Palestinian Authority (PA) plans to develop a rational transportation network with connections between the major urban centers and with Israel, Jordan, and Gaza. Prefeasibility studies have been conducted for an airport and for rail and road networks in the West Bank, but according to the PA Ministry of Transport plans have been held back by the lack of access to Area C.

Movement

As it is, the movement of goods and people is restricted considerably by today's system of barriers, checkpoints, and movement permits. While there has been an easing of the barriers to movement within the West Bank in recent years, the system of internal movement restrictions continues to fragment the West Bank, largely on account of restrictions to movement in and across Area C.[1] At the end of 2012, 60 Palestinian communities were still compelled to use detours that are two to five times longer than the direct route to the closest city.[2] The additional costs attributable to the time of travel brought on by travel restrictions on three major routes in the West Bank alone has been calculated at USD 185 million per annum.[3] Using different methods, Cali and Miaari (2013) estimate that the costs of West Bank movement restrictions to the Palestinian labor market totaled some USD 229 million in 2007.

Water and Wastewater

Many communities in Area C are not connected to the Palestinian water network and face the higher prices of using water tankers.[4] The price of this water also depends on the costs of transport, which are often increased by checkpoints and other barriers to movement. These communities are concentrated in the northern and southern parts of the West Bank, especially in the Hebron, Jenin, and Tubas governorates.[5] The quality of this water is also poor, with consequent negative health impacts[6] and associated economic losses.[7]

The restrictions on accessing water in and across Area C also impact the main economic sectors. Chapter 2 has described the impact on agricultural potential of a lack of adequate water supplies—but the shortages and expense of water also constrain the industrial sector, as the most recent World Bank Investment Climate Assessment indicates.[8] The experience of the emergent city of Rawabi mentioned in chapter 2 shows how difficult it can be for new developments to access adequate water supplies when lines need to cross Area C.

Wastewater treatment is affected by the restrictions on infrastructure development in Area C. There is an insufficient number of Palestinian treatment plants to handle the wastewater of the West Bank, resulting in water being treated inside Israel or in Israeli plants in the West Bank[9]—and then reused by Israel. The treatment costs are apparently deducted by Government of Israel (GoI) from the Palestinian tax clearances without accounting for any reuse.[10] At the same time, Palestinians have to purchase water from the Israeli water company Mekorot to help satisfy their water requirements—in 2012, 51 MCM for a total cost of around USD 37 million.[11]

Telecommunications

The indirect impact of restrictions on the quality and cost of the telecommunications infrastructure is also noteworthy. A 2005 study on the importance of infrastructure for growth in Africa concluded that a 1 percent increase in investment in telecoms infrastructure could lead to a 0.19 percent growth in gross domestic product (GDP).[12] As figure 3.1 shows, linkages between the telecommunications sector and other sectors of the Palestinian economy are sizeable, since roughly 30 percent of telecommunications output is used as production inputs in other

Figure 3.1 Telecommunications Sector Output Purchased by Other Sectors of the Economy

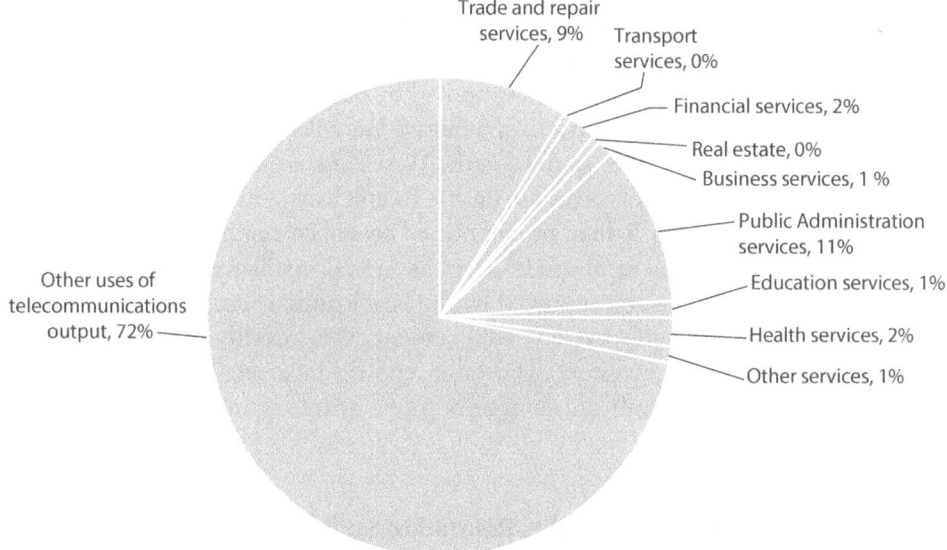

Source: PCBS, preliminary supply and use tables (based on 2004 data).

sectors. As discussed in chapter 2, the quality of telecommunications services legally accessible to Palestinians is suboptimal, and this drives up costs; one of the Palestinian mobile providers reports that its consumer prices are on average 15–16 percent higher than if the company were able to operate in Area C. According to the International Telecommunication Union (ITU), the monthly price of fixed broadband in Palestinian territories, after factoring in purchasing power parity, is almost 40 percent higher than the average in the Middle East and North Africa region.[13] Although not all of these additional costs should be attributed to Israeli restrictions, a significant part can be.

Institutional Infrastructure

Restrictions on access to Area C limit Palestinian banks' ability to develop operations there. Palestinian banks find it extremely difficult to expand their customer base in Area C because licenses to build branches or install automated teller machines (ATMs) are almost impossible to obtain.[14] This reduces the Area C Palestinian population's access to finance. Palestinian banks report that even if approval to establish banking facilities in Area C were granted, they would still be hesitant to go forward because of the law enforcement difficulties in Area C, where the PA is unable to carry out effective policing.[15] Some local banks do finance commercial activities in Area C, but these loans must either be guaranteed by third parties or collateralized by assets in Areas A and B. Banks are highly unlikely to accept Area C land as collateral due to the lengthy approval process and uncertainties associated with foreclosure in Area C—including the possibility that land could end up being sold to non-Palestinian buyers.[16] Since Area C represents the bulk of West Bank land, this has had a negative effect on the growth of West Bank credit. According to Palestinian Central Bureau of Statistics (PCBS), almost 98 percent of Palestinian establishments refrain from requesting bank credit because of difficult collateral requirements imposed by banks.[17]

Restrictions on access to Area C also impede law enforcement in large parts of the West Bank.[18] All 64 police stations in the West Bank are situated in Areas A and B. Palestinian civil police forces are unable to efficiently enforce the law in those parts of Areas A and B that are connected to police centers by roads passing through Area C. Movement inside or across Area C involves a written coordination request that must be approved by the Israeli authorities, which may hinder timely policing and effective law enforcement. This inability to provide proper policing discourages investors, who often end up incurring extra maintenance costs to make up for theft and damage, or hiring private security agents to protect their investments.

Secondary Costs and Benefits Related to Spillover Effects

Addressing the constraints to the growth of the sectors analyzed in chapter 2 would have sizeable effects on the demand for output in other related sectors. Despite the relative lack of diversification of the Palestinian economy and the underdeveloped nature of its domestic supply chains, the linkages that exist are important. Tourism, for example, is closely connected with agriculture and food production, transport and communications, construction, and other service and industrial sectors, as figure 3.2 shows. The cost of the intermediary inputs produced by other sectors and used in the tourism industry exceeds the value added in the tourism sector per se.[19] In addition to this, investments in tourism facilities and

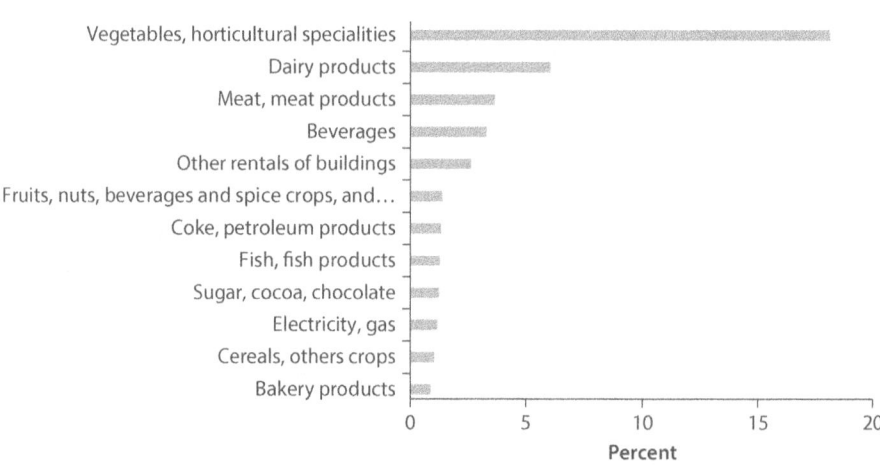

Figure 3.2 Palestinian Tourism's Reliance on Inputs from Agriculture and Agroprocessing

Source: PCBS, preliminary supply and use tables (based on 2004 data).

its accompanying infrastructure would give a strong boost to the construction sector, while the revenues earned through tourism would result in expenditures in other sectors of the economy. The aggregated opportunity cost of the absence of tourism activity in Area C—and the corresponding benefits of rectifying this situation—would substantially exceed the potential value added to the tourism sector alone. Various studies from other countries suggest a multiplier effect ranging from 1 to 3.5.[20]

Similarly, the suppression of the construction sector caused by the restrictions has an indirect impact on other sectors though backward linkages. This sector is a large user of aggregates, and interviews with West Bank crushers confirm that part of the crisis of their sector is the result of anemic demand for construction. The sector also uses local stone and marble, which involves quarrying, cutting, and polishing. The construction sector is, moreover, an intense user of transport and logistics services. The Rawabi project illustrates the importance of these backward linkages. The project has created employment for up to 4,500 people in all, the majority from sectors such as quarrying, transport, logistics, security, and real estate services.

Potential Indirect Benefits

In aggregate, the indirect effects associated with the potential output expansion in the sectors reviewed in chapter 2 would be equivalent to 50 percent of that output expansion. The multiplier effect was calculated on the basis of Supply and Uses Tables for the Palestinian economy recently prepared by PCBS from 2004 National Accounts data. The process involved estimating the demand for intermediary inputs from other sectors of the Palestinian economy generated by the expansion of each of the sectors profiled in chapter 2. The sum of these intermediary input requirements was then multiplied by a weighted average ratio of value added to output for each of the sectors. The structure of the economy has changed since 2004, and the intersectoral linkages have also changed since then—but not so much as to invalidate the estimates. The overall multiplier effect emerging from this exercise is 1.5—and, since general equilibrium modeling techniques could not be used, is likely to be an underestimate (additional third-round benefits and induced effects could not be captured).

In sum, the total potential value added (direct and indirect as a result of the alleviation of today's restrictions on access to, and activity and production in Area C is likely to amount to about USD 3.4 billion—or 35 percent of Palestinian GDP in 2011.

The impact of this increase in value added on employment and poverty would be large. The International Monetary Fund (IMF) has estimated that a relationship between growth and employment is almost one-to-one.[21] Thus, an increase in GDP of 35 percent, *ceteris paribus*, would lead to an equivalent increase in employment. However, since this increase in GDP would require major structural changes in the Palestinian economy, the relationship estimated by the IMF may not hold. Furthermore, the effect of this increase in GDP on unemployment would depend on the time it would take for it to happen, given the natural growth of the working-age population. However, even if the relationship between GDP growth and employment were to become significantly weaker, the increase in the number of jobs caused by a 35 percent increase in GDP would still be quite substantial. Furthermore, as the World Bank's analysis shows, poverty rate among unemployed measured in 2009 was 36 percent and only 17 percent for employed (2.1 times higher).[22] Thus, the large potential increase in employment emanating from the lifting of Area C restrictions would put a considerable dent in the level of poverty in Palestinian territories.

Potential Fiscal Benefits

Tapping this potential output could dramatically improve the PA's fiscal position. Even without any improvements in the efficiency of tax collection, at the current rate of tax/GDP of 20 percent, the additional tax revenues associated with an increase in GDP would amount to some USD 800 million. Assuming that expenditures remain at the same level, this extra resource would notionally cut the fiscal deficit by half—significantly reducing the need for donor recurrent budget support (table 3.1).[23] This major improvement in fiscal sustainability would in turn generate significant positive reputational benefits for the PA and would considerably enhance investor confidence.

Table 3.1 Potential Revenue and Deficit Reduction
In thousands of USD

	Status Quo	Potential
PA revenues	1,974.6	2,758.8
PA expenditures	3,362.7	3,362.7
PA deficit	−1,388.1	−603.9

Source: Palestinian Ministry of Finance 2012 fiscal data and World Bank staff calculations.
Note: PA = Palestinian Authority.

Notes

1. United Nations Office for the Coordination of Humanitarian Affairs (UN OCHA), 2012. "West Bank Movement and Access Update."
2. Interviews by the World Bank (2007) confirm that an important part of the reason behind repressed production and sales relates to the difficulty of moving between areas. In 2000, nearly 60 percent of firms made a significant share of their sales outside their home town; by 2005, this had fallen to around 40 percent. See World Bank, 2007. "Movement and Access Restrictions in the West Bank: Uncertainty and Inefficiency in the Palestinian Economy."
3. PA Ministry of National Economy and Arij, 2011. "The Economic Costs of the Israeli Occupation for the Occupied Palestinian Territory."
4. Some communities connected to the network also have to resort to tankered water due to insufficient supply.
5. Palestinian Water Authority, 2012. "National Water Strategy for Palestine."
6. World Bank, 2009. "Assessment of Restrictions on Palestinian Water Sector Development." Sector Note.
7. Looking at the nature and cost of the medical treatments involved, and without accounting for any losses of adult productivity, it has been estimated that the annual cost of the health impacts of poor water and sanitation on children aged five or less is c. USD 20 million. See World Bank, 2009. "Assessment of Restrictions on Palestinian Water Sector Development." Sector Note: on the basis of Glover, S., and A. Hunter, 2010. "Meeting Future Palestinian Water Needs," Palestine Economic Research Institute (MAS).
8. World Bank, 2009. "Assessment of Restrictions on Palestinian Water Sector Development." Sector Note.
9. In 2011, around 15 MCM of wastewater was collected from the West Bank and treated in wastewater plants inside Israel.
10. Palestinian Water Authority, 2012. "National Water Strategy for Palestine."
11. Ibid.
12. Estache, et al., 2005. "How Much Does Infrastructure Matter to Growth in Sub-Saharan Africa?" Working Paper.
13. One month of fixed broadband costs Palestinians USD 39, while it costs Lebanese USD 27, Egyptians USD 17, Jordanians USD 26, and Yemenis USD 18.
14. Based on interviews conducted with two large Palestinian banks.
15. The manager of a local bank reports that his company wanted to place ATM machines in Area C, but no insurance company was willing to cover the machines against theft and vandalism.
16. Any application to use a piece of land in Area C as loan collateral has to be approved by the Israeli Civil Administration. Local banks report that the approval process is time consuming taking on average between 1.5 and 2 months, while the time required to obtain approval by the Palestinian Land Authority for land in Areas A and B does not usually exceed one week. Local banks are also hesitant to accept Area C land as collateral because the foreclosure process can be difficult—given that Palestinian law enforcement agents find it difficult to operate in Area C. Furthermore, foreclosed land in Area C has to be offered for sale in auctions that are managed by the Israeli Civil Administration, which raises concerns over the loss of Palestinian land to

non-Palestinian buyers. In practice local banks have preferred not to foreclose such properties, and have ended up bearing the losses resulting from bad loans collateralized by Area C land.
17. PCBS, "Survey of the Perceptions of Owners/Managers of Active Industrial Enterprises Regarding the Economic Situation, Q1 2013."
18. Information collected through meeting with experts who have conducted field research on the access and movement restrictions applicable to the Palestinian civil police.
19. PCBS, 2004. "Supply and Uses Tables," preliminary results.
20. Horváth, Endre, and Douglas C. Frechtling, 1999. "Estimating the Multiplier Effects of Tourism Expenditures on a Local Economy through a Regional Input-Output Model."
21. The relationship was estimated by the IMF in their 2012 report titled, *West Bank and Gaza: Labor Market Trends, Growth and Unemployment.*
22. *Coping with Conflict: Poverty and Inclusion in the West Bank and Gaza*, World Bank, 2011.
23. In reality, the lifting of restrictions on Area C would probably lead to an increase in public investments to develop infrastructure there. These investments would increase public expenditures, but they would also contribute to growth and the net effect is uncertain. Thus, for the sake of this report no change in the level of public expenditures associated with the lifting of Area C restrictions was assumed.

APPENDIX A

Methodological Notes

Given that Area C (a) provides contiguity to the economic space of the West Bank and (b) is the most resource-abundant region of the West Bank, the importance of access to economic activity in Area C for the Palestinian economy is widely recognized. The utilization of this potential for the Palestinian economy has been made impossible by various restrictions, which were explained in detail in previous sections of this report. Thus, though recognized, the size of this potential is not self-evident. Moreover, a systematic effort has apparently not been made earlier to evaluate this potential. The completion of such an evaluation has been the main objective of this report.

To accomplish this objective it was necessary to construct a counterfactual world without the restrictions that currently preclude most of economic activity by Palestinian agents in Area C. Furthermore, to measure this potential, it also had to be assumed that other restrictions on economic activity, such as those that impede free movement of people, goods, and capital have been lifted. In other words, a counterfactual world with a reasonably sound investment climate has been created for the West Bank. Granted these assumptions, two main approaches were employed to accomplish the above-stated objective of this report: First, to the extent that data were available and adequate counterfactuals could be constructed, this potential was quantified in terms of value added that could be generated for the Palestinian economy. Unfortunately, robust counterfactuals can be challenging to define and even more challenging to support with adequate data that would enable one to measure a perceived economic potential. Thus, in some cases, the potential has been qualitatively illustrated by analogy rather than quantified. Consequently, the quantified potential presented in figures in this report is thought to be an underestimate of the true potential contribution of Area C to the Palestinian economy. This assertion is also accentuated by the fact that relatively conservative assumptions were made in order to quantify the potential where such quantification was deemed possible.

Furthermore, different techniques were utilized to construct what were considered to be the most appropriate counterfactuals for each of the five sectors, whose potential has been evaluated in this report. The choice of the technique employed for each sector was made with what were considered to be the best proxies for the potential being measured and based on data availability. The technique employed to construct the quantifiable counterfactual for each of the sectors along with that used to estimate the multiplier effect is explained in detail below.

Agriculture

For the agriculture sector an evaluation is made of incremental value added that could be generated if the restrictions were lifted to allow investments by Palestinian economic agents to freely produce agricultural products in Area C and to be able to freely sell them in the Palestinian market and abroad. The following assumptions are crucial to this evaluation: (a) incremental land surface in Area C that could be cultivated by Palestinian farmers and (b) value of output per dunum of cultivated land.

The computation of the potential value of incremental agricultural production in Area C is obtained through several steps. The first is to estimate the average production value per dunum for each of the two principle farming methods (irrigated vs. rain fed). This is done using the latest available data for agricultural production for the Palestinian territory (that is the agricultural statistics 2007/08).[1] Using these data, which reflect the Palestinian agriculture productivity for each of the two principle farming methods, the production value per dunum by crop and by farming method is computed (see tables B.1, B.2 and B.3 in appendix B, which report the three major categories of crops, fruit trees, field crops, and vegetables). This method allows the estimation of the average production value per dunum separately for irrigated and rain-fed land weighting each crop by its importance in terms of production value so as to reflect the current cropping patterns (that is mix of crops planted).[2] Unsurprisingly, the difference in productivity between the two farming methods is huge: The average value of production on irrigated land is USD 2,344 against USD 162 on rain-fed land. This difference already suggests the potential for agricultural expansion through the intensive margin (that is increasing irrigation). In the absence of more recent price data for individual crops, these values (based on 2007 data) are then inflated by the price inflation of agriculture between 2007 and 2011 (equal to 15.52 percent according to the Palestinian Central Bureau of Statistics [PCBS]) to obtain the value of USD 2,708 for the value of irrigated agriculture and USD 187 for rain-fed agriculture in 2011.

The second step in evaluating the potential consists of estimating the size of the land which can be potentially used for agriculture in Area C. Land Research Center (LRC [2010]) estimates that the potential agricultural land which is suitable for reclamation in Area C is 303,763 dunum. The 187,000 dunums directly used by the settlements, half of which is for agricultural cultivation, have been excluded from the calculations of additional cultivable land. The potential additional cultivable land in Area C, estimated in this way, amounts to 376,666 dunum of effective cropping area, which takes into account the adjustment for multiseasonal farming.[3] In order to obtain the total potential arable land in Area C, this figure needs to be added to the land which is already cultivated in Area C and which is, however, not explicitly recorded by the PCBS. The size of that land is obtained by

Methodological Notes

multiplying the share of the West Bank cultivated land located in Area C (45.8 percent according to LRC, 2010), by the total land cultivated in the West Bank (1.7 million dunum according to PCBS, 2009a).[4] The total land thus estimated that is currently cultivated in Area C is 776,477 dunum (of which 67,919 dunum is irrigated, or 45.8 percent of West Bank irrigated land). Adding the additional cultivable land and the land currently cultivated by Palestinians in Area C yields the total land potentially cultivable in Area C, which is 1.153 million dunum.

The third step consists of identifying how much of this land is potentially irrigable, as the productivity of irrigated and rain-fed land is very different. This computation relies on the estimated potentially irrigable land in the Palestinian territory, equal to 745,000 dunum, as reported in Glover and Hunter (2010) and confirmed by PCBS and the Palestinian Ministry of Agriculture. Turning this estimate into the effective cropping area and discounting the irrigated area in Gaza (from PCBS, 2009a) gives a total of 808,387 dunum of effective cropping area potentially irrigable in the West Bank.[5] Multiplying this estimate by the share of Area C in the potentially cultivable land in the West Bank computed by LRC (2010), that is, 48.8 percent, gives a total of 394,320 dunum of potentially irrigable land in Area C.

Using the estimates of potentially irrigable and potentially cultivable lands in Area C and the production value per dunum of irrigated and rain-fed agriculture computed above, it is estimated that the potential value of agricultural production in Area C is equal to 394,320 dunum × USD 2708/dunum = USD 1.068 billion of irrigated agriculture, and 754,000 dunum × USD 187/dunum = USD 141 million for rain-fed agriculture. Thus, the total potential value of cultivation in Area C amounts to USD 1.209 billion.

Then, since some agriculture activity is conducted currently in Area C despite the restrictions, the incremental value of production is equal to the difference between the total potential value of production estimated above and the level of current production in Area C: USD1.209 billion - USD 316 million = USD 893. Based on the ratio of agriculture value added to the value of output that is observed in the Palestinian national accounts (78 percent), one can calculate the potential incremental value added as follows: USD 893 × 78% = USD 698.

In addition to estimating the value generated through cultivation, the value of rangeland has also been estimated by The Palestinian Ministry of Agriculture (2012) and can be added to the estimated value of agricultural production above.[6] The value was estimated based on the savings on the cost of fodder that the herders could realize should they have access to this grazing land.[7] In particular, the estimation is based on the weight of the dry matter per square meter of rangeland and the average grazing capacity (1.22 per dunum per month) of natural rangelands using land cover assessment and vegetation density analysis. The cost of fodder was estimated based on the assumption that cattle grazing in the rangeland would provide a part of the daily need of fodder (replacing the barley) for the number of grazing months with a cost that is estimated at NIS 1.5/day/head. This calculation puts the total potential value of rangeland at USD 7.061 million per year, of which USD 6 million amounts to the foregone value due to the restrictions. Thus, the incremental value added that could potentially be generated in the agriculture sector following the removal of the restrictions can be calculated by adding the annual agriculture output estimated above and the incremental rangeland output:

USD 698 million + USD 6 million = USD 704 million.

Stone Mining and Quarrying

The potential incremental output of stone production in Area C was calculated as follows: Given that Area C comprises about 61 percent of the West Bank territory and it is much more sparsely populated than Areas A and B (the latter are mostly urban and peri-urban), it was assumed that at least 61 percent of all stone deposits lie in Area C.[8] Currently, only 70 of around 300 Palestinian stone mining and quarrying operations are located in Area C and only a handful of them operate legally and without interruptions, as discussed in chapter 2. Nevertheless, assuming that the number of quarries per square kilometer of land that can be opened in Area C is equivalent to the number of those currently operating in Areas A and B per square kilometer, one can calculate that 275 new quarries could be opened in Area C. The number of potential new quarries was calculated as follows: Currently, in Areas A and B, there are an estimated 230 quarries (300 in total minus 70 operated in Area C). Given that Areas A and B consist of 39 percent of the West Bank, with equal density of quarries across the entire West Bank, one can calculate the number of potential quarries for the whole West Bank as 230/39% = 590. Thus the incremental, number of quarries in Area C would be equal to 590 - 300 = 290; Assuming the current value added generated per stone quarry (including value added generated through stone processing) and assuming equal average production per quarry, one can easily calculate the forgone value added at USD 229 million. The existing 300 quarries and stone processing operations generate a value added of USD 250 million. Two hundred and ninety new quarries and stone processing operations, assuming the same level of productivity, could generate: 290/300 × USD250 million = USD241 million.[9]

Minerals and Cosmetics

Since as of yet no investments have been allowed to develop a Palestinian Dead Sea minerals processing industry, the counterfactual was developed based on the equivalent industries in Israel and Jordan as explained in the main text of this report. The value added was calculated as the average of value added generated by these industries in Israel and Jordan. Provided that, in particular in Israel, a number of products have been developed whose production is not strictly dependent on the access to the Dead Sea mineral resources, the estimates generated for this report exclude the value of such sophisticated products. Instead, the estimates presented herein assume the extraction of Dead Sea minerals and the production of less sophisticated derivative products (for example bromine-based flame retardants).

Methodological Notes

The data to calculate the relevant value added generated by the relevant Israeli and Jordanian companies were primarily obtained from the public financial statements of those companies for 2012. The estimates of value added were made separately for the potash production on one hand and the production of bromine, bromine derivatives, and magnesium on the other hand.

The value added for potash production in Israel was estimated as follows: Total Israeli Chemicals Ltd (ICL) revenues from potash sales in 2012 were reduced by revenues earned based on potash production outside of Israel to obtain potash revenues generated in Israel alone. The ratio of total potash sales/potash sales based on Dead Sea production (Israel) was multiplied by the operating profit resulting from total potash sales. Employment compensation and amortization costs were added to the above estimate. These were calculated based on the available data for ICL employment compensation and amortization costs, by multiplying each of those numbers with the share of Dead Sea Potash revenues to total ICL revenues. This is a simplification as different segments of ICL's business are not equally labor intensive. However, these two figures make up only about 25 percent of the total value added, which would mute the impact of errors in the allocation of labor costs on the overall estimate. Details on how the value added for potash production in Israel and Jordan has been calculated are shown in the table A.1. Then, the potential for the Palestinian potash industry has been estimated as the average of the Israeli and Jordanian industries, which is equal to USD 642 million.

Table A.1 Calculation of Value Added for Potash Production

Israel	USD 000	Jordan	USD 000
Total ICL potash sales	2198	Total potash sales by Arab Potash Company	762.8
Iberpotash	387		
CPL	290.7		
Dead Sea	1520.3		
Dead Sea/Total potash sales	69%		
Dead Sea Potash sales/Total ICL sales	23%		
Operating profit from potash sales	996.5	Operating profit from potash sales	265.1
Share of operating profit attributable to Dead Sea Potash	689.2		
ICL depreciation and amortization expenses	287		
Dead Sea share of amortization and depreciation	65.4	APC's depreciation and amortization expenses	5.9
Total employee compensation	789		
Dead Sea share of employee compensation expenses	179.8	APC's employee compensation	79
Value added based on Dead Sea Potash extraction	934.4151	Value added from potash production in Jordan	349.962

Source: Israel Chemicals, ltd (ICL), Arab Potash Company (APC), and World Bank staff calculations.
Note: APC = Arab Potash Company.

The same methodology was applied to calculate the revenues generated based on the sales of bromine and magnesia products produced by ICL IP and Jordan Bromine Company in Jordan. The main additional assumption made for ICL was that 80 percent of its sales revenues were based on bromine, magnesia, and derivatives thereof, all based on the extraction of these minerals from the Dead Sea. Furthermore, since only revenue data for the Jordan Bromine Company were available to the authors, the ratio of value added to revenues was calculated based on the Israeli data and applied to the Jordanian revenues to obtain the value added generated through bromine production in Jordan.

As explained in the text, due to the challenge in constructing a reasonable counterfactual for the Palestinian Dead Sea–based cosmetics industry, efforts were not made to quantify this potential. Thus, the estimate of incremental value added that could potentially be generated in the Stone, Minerals, and Cosmetics industries is considered to be a relatively conservative one as it excludes estimates of potential value added that could be generated in the stone aggregates industry and the cosmetics industry, although both appear to have significant potential.

Construction and Real Estate Services

Estimating the impact of the inability to operate in Area C on value added in the housing sector (or conversely measuring the potential value added impact of their removal) required several steps to be taken. First, as elaborated in detail in the main text of the report, it was established that Area C restrictions, through constraining supply, were affecting the price of the construction land in Area C. Second, the impact of higher land prices on housing prices, *ceteris paribus*, was calculated. This calculation is performed along similar lines to the differences-in-differences estimation, as follows: First, a difference between overall consumer price index (CPI) and housing prices for the period 1996–2012 was calculated for the West Bank (ΔWB). The same price differential was calculated for Gaza (ΔG). The difference between ΔWB and ΔG indicates that the current restrictions on construction activity in Area C have likely caused an increase in housing prices by around 24 percent in the West Bank. This, of course, is on top of the general increase in prices and accounting for the potentially different evolution of house prices vis-à-vis the rest of the consumption basket. The mechanism of this additional price increase in the West Bank can be explained as an inward parallel shift of the supply curve caused by the increase in the price for one of the important inputs in the production of housing (that is, the price of construction land).

To estimate how the 24 percent increase in housing prices has affected the quantity of housing produced, one has to have an estimate of the demand curve for housing in the West Bank. In order to calculate the effect on the quantity of housing units developed, the price elasticity of demand for housing is needed. However, no such estimates could be found for the West Bank. Nevertheless, the elasticity computed by Malpezzi and Mayo (1987) for the Egyptian city of Beni Suef can serve as a proxy for demand elasticity in the West Bank. This is one of the rare price elasticities of demand for housing available in developing countries.

Methodological Notes

In addition it has the advantage of referring to a city of comparable size to the main West Bank cities and is located in the Arab Republic of Egypt, which has a similar culture and level of economic development to the Palestinian territory. These features minimize the possible bias deriving from noneconomic determinants of housing demand. These estimated elasticities for Beni Suef range between –0.76 and –1.02.

Then, taking the simple average of these two elasticity estimates and applying it to the estimated price effect of the Area C restrictions yields a drop in the market clearing quantity for residential housing of 21.7 percent. Conversely, the lifting of the Area C restrictions would be expected to lead to a 21.7 percent increase in the quantity of residential housing constructed in the West Bank; but, since the price would also decline by 24 percent, the total value of gross output of construction and real estate services would be similar to the, *ex ante* value, with the Area C restrictions (only 3 percent lower).[10] However, the value added would be substantially higher with the lifting of the restrictions, as the restrictions lead to an increase in the cost of an intermediary input shifting the supply curve, and the value added per unit of housing produced is virtually unchanged before and after the restrictions (Figure A.1). Thus, once the restrictions are lifted and the quantity of housing increases, value added is increased in the same proportion as the increase in quantity of housing produced, which as shown above, has been estimated at 21.7 percent. Since the value added of housing and real estate activities in 2011 amounted to USD 1.103 billion, it can be estimated that, in the absence of Area C restrictions, the incremental value added would have amounted to: USD1.103 × 27.7% = USD 239 million.

Figure A.1 The Effects of The Restrictions on Price and Quantity of Construction

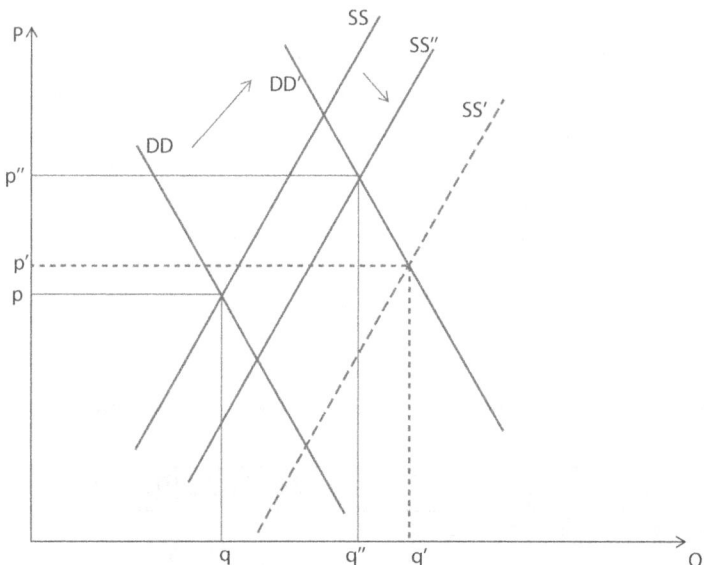

Source: Authors' elaboration.

Telecommunications

To estimate the direct impact of the inability to operate in Area C on the value added of the telecommunications sector, an effort was made to account for the impact of restrictions on revenues of the Palestinian telecommunications companies on one hand and their impact on the cost these companies face (for intermediary inputs) on the other hand. Thus, lost value added is equal to the sum of pretax revenues forgone and costs incurred due to the inability to operate in Area C. The following discussion describes how all revenue and cost items that were included in the calculation of the sector's foregone value added were quantified.

Mobile Operators (Jawwal and Wataniya)

Revenues

Potential revenues lost due to the inability to serve customers in Area C. Restrictions on building infrastructure in Area C limit the Palestinian mobile operators' ability to serve many of the 180,000 residents who live in this area, leading to potential revenue losses. Based on a penetration rate of 81 percent for mobiles in the West Bank, and given that the average revenue per user (ARPU) for Palestinian mobile holders is (USD 12.44) per month, these revenue losses are estimated at USD 18 million per year (table A.2).

Costs

Extra costs for serving customers in Areas A and B as a result of restrictions on Area C. The inability of the Palestinian mobile operators to build infrastructure in Area C increases the cost of serving customers in Areas A and B as it forces the companies to lay a larger number of towers in suboptimal locations in Areas A and B to provide good coverage. This leads to efficiency losses estimated by the operators at USD 11.5 million per year.

Extra cost related to having core equipment outside Palestinian territories (table A.3). Due to restrictions on importing equipment, the mobile operators established their cores (network centres) outside Palestinian territories. To establish a transmission path between the local switches and the cores placed outside, the operators had to lay fiber lines that extend through Area C. Because the Government of Israel (GoI) would not give permission to construct such lines in Area C, one operator was forced to contract an Israeli firm to establish, operate, and maintain the links. Fees to the Israeli company amount to USD 8.75 per year.

Table A.2 Annual Potential Revenues Lost by the Palestinian Mobile Operators Due to the Restrictions

Revenue	Amount (USD thousand)
Potential revenues lost due to the inability to serve customers in Area C	18,245

Source: World Bank staff calculations based on data from Palestinian mobile operators.

Methodological Notes

Table A.3 Annual Costs Incurred by the Palestinian Mobile Operators Due to the Inability to Freely Operate in Area C

Cost	Amount (USD thousand)
Extra costs for serving customers in Areas A and B as a result of restrictions on Area C	11,541
Extra cost related to having core equipment outside Palestinian territories, of which:	9,860[a]
Fees to the Israeli company to establish, operate, and maintain network links in Area C	8,750
Potential revenues lost due to slow repair of network faults in Area C	1,110
Total annual cost	21,401

Source: World Bank staff calculations based on data from Palestinian mobile operators.

a. This figure is underestimated as only one of the mobile operators provided estimates for extra cost related to having core equipment outside Ramallah.

In addition, the operator's inability to access Area C makes it prone to revenue losses because it cannot guarantee prompt action by the Israeli firm in case a fault occurs in any of the links there. This is estimated at about USD 1.11 million in potential revenue losses annually.

Landline Provider (Paltel)

Revenues

Potential revenues lost due to the inability to serve customers in Area C. The company currently provides landline and asymmetric digital subscriber line (ADSL) services to 8,000 out of the 16,300[11] households that represent the respective market in Area C. The company estimates that an opportunity to serve these potential customers could generate an additional USD 2.15 million per year in revenues (Table A.4), based on a household penetration rate of 10 percent and assuming that the annual ARPU for landline and ADSL in Area C is the same as in the rest of the Palestinian territories.[12]

Restrictions on building infrastructure in Area C limit the company's ability to upgrade the internet speed of users connected through infrastructure in this area. Given that the price of Internet service is directly correlated to its speed, this represents another lost opportunity that, according to the operator, could generate around USD 234,000 per year.

Potential revenue lost due to delays in repairing network faults in Area C. Due to difficulties in getting permission from the Israeli Authorities to carry out regular maintenance work or network faults repair in Area C, landlines and ADSL lines that are connected through infrastructure in Area C face disconnects of a total of 14.17 days every year, collectively. This leads to lost minutes that translate into a potential revenue loss for the operator estimated at about USD 141,000 per year.

Revenues forgone to Israeli competition. Competition created by the Israeli firms in the Palestinian market also leads to potential revenue losses for the landline operator. On the whole sale level and based on a recent estimate for Internet capacity needed by the local ISPs but not received from the local operator and the average unit price of Internet, it is estimated that this competition leads to annual potential revenue losses of about USD 1.18 million. On the retail level, a recent survey by the operator shows that the number of Palestinian households that currently receive Internet from Israeli firms is estimated at about 18,865. Given that the monthly ARPU for Internet in Palestinian territories is USD 14.76, it is estimated that potential revenues lost by the operator are about USD 3.34 million per year.

Costs

Extra costs for serving customers in Areas A and B as a result of restrictions on Area C. The inability to develop infrastructure in Area C is also associated with higher costs for serving customers in Areas A and B as the company is forced to lay down its fiber network through longer detours bypassing Area C. The company reports that this raises its overall cost by USD 148 thousand per year (Table A.5.).

Cost of high churn rate among customers connected through infrastructure in Area C. The company finds it extremely difficult to get permission from the Israeli Authorities to carry out regular maintenance work or network faults repair in Area C, and therefore places that are connected through fiber in Area C suffer from low-quality service and long disconnects which lead to high churn rates among customers. Based on a monthly ADSL ARPU of USD 14.76 and an annual average of 718 cancelled subscriptions, this is estimated to lead to USD 127 thousand in lost revenues per year.

The cost of hiring an Israeli company to access and fix network faults in Area C. To avoid delays in obtaining a permission to operate in Area C, the Palestinian operator often resorts to hiring an Israeli maintenance company to fix network faults there. This is estimated to cost around USD 450,000 per year.

Copper thefts in Area C. The company's network segments in Area C suffer from frequent actions of theft and vandalism due to the lack of security there. It

Table A.4 Annual Potential Revenues Lost by the Palestinian Landline Operator Due to the Area C Restrictions

Revenue	Amount (USD thousand)
Potential revenues lost due to the inability to serve customers in Area C	2,145
Potential revenues lost due to the operator's inability to upgrade Internet speed for customers connected through infrastructure in Area C	234
Potential revenue lost due to delays in repairing network faults in Area C	141
Revenues forgone to Israeli competition, of which	4,519
Wholesale competition	1,177
Retail competition	3,342
Total annual potential revenue lost	7,039

Source: World Bank staff calculations based on Paletel data.

Table A.5 Annual Costs Incurred by the Palestinian Landline Operator Due to the Area C Restrictions

Cost	Amount (USD thousand)
Extra costs for serving customers in Areas A and B as a result of restrictions on Area C	148
Cost of high churn rate among customers connected through infrastructure in Area C	127
Hiring an Israeli company to access and fix network faults in Area C	450
Copper thefts in Area C	340
Additional investment to protect network segments in Area C	117
Total annual cost	1,182

Source: World Bank staff calculations based on Paletel data.

is estimated that these incidents cost the company around USD 340,000 per year mainly due to the cost of additional fiber and copper needed to relink the damaged network segments.

Additional investment to protect network segments in Area C. In order to try and protect its network in Area C, the company applies additional security measures there such as building concrete structures around the telecom lines and hiring security services to guard the infrastructure. This additional cost is estimated at about USD 117,000 per year.

Annual potential revenues lost by the mobile operators and the landline company quantified in this section amount to USD 25,284 million, while annual costs incurred total USD 22,583. Based on these figures, the foregone value added for the sector is estimated to be USD 47,867 million.

Tourism

To estimate the size of potential Dead Sea tourism investments on the Palestinian side, Israel's Dead Sea tourism industry was used to construct the counterfactual, as it is deemed to be a very good proxy for the potential being estimated in this report. The vast majority of Israeli hotels and resorts along the Dead Sea are located in an area of southern Dead Sea shore that stretches about 6 kilometers in length. The Palestinian Dead Sea Coast based on the 1967 borders is about 40 kilometers long and offers the potential to build resorts with accommodation capacity that is at least as large as that developed along the Israeli Dead Sea shore. While of course not all of the 40 kilometers of the Dead Sea shore that lies in Area C of the West Bank is suitable for resort development, a very conservative assumption would be that at least 6 kilometers (15 percent of total length) could be developed into resorts similar to those in Israel and Jordan. The Dead Sea shore along the West Bank, currently designated as Area C, has similar characteristics (in terms of tourism potential) to those of the Dead Sea shore in Israel; thus, *ceteris paribus*, one can assume the potential tourism demand to correspond to that on the Israeli side of the Dead Sea. Thus, if resort capacity was developed on only 15 percent of the total Dead Sea shore length along the West Bank, room capacity could amount at least to 4,000 units, equivalent to the current room capacity on the Israeli side of the Dead Sea shore.[13]

Since the data for total tourism value added for Israel are available, and so is the share of Dead Sea tourism employment in total tourism employment in Israel, assuming the same labor productivity across the industry in Israel, we can easily estimate the value added generated by Dead Sea tourism in Israel at: Dead Sea tourism employment/total tourism employment (2010) × tourism value added in Israel (2010) = 2.8 percent × USD 4.5 billion = USD 126 million. Assuming labor productivity equivalent to that in the Israeli tourism industry, the opportunity cost in terms of direct employment would be about 2,900 workers.

The estimated value-added potential of USD 126 is probably conservative. This estimate doesn't include the potential of developing other tourism sites and products in Area C, despite the fact that this potential is also deemed significant as discussed in the main text of this report.

Estimating the Size of the Multiplier Effect

As discussed in chapter 3 of the report, indirect effects of Area C restrictions are thought to be quite significant. These costs can be classified into two essential groups: costs related to the negative impact of Area C restrictions on the development of both physical and institutional infrastructure, as well as the costs related to the spillover effects stemming from interlinkages among different sectors of the Palestinian economy. The first group is, in particular, challenging to quantify and no attempt has been made to do so in this report. The most standard way to estimate the size of the spillover effect would be to build an adequate general equilibrium model of the Palestinian economy, relying on the data from the supply and uses tables in the Palestinian national accounts. Unfortunately, such a model does not exist yet and its development is beyond the scope of this report.

Nevertheless, the authors have worked with the data from the Supply and Uses Tables for the Palestinian economy, which were recently produced by PCBS (preliminary estimates for 2004) to produce an estimate of the multiplier effect that would be associated with the estimated potential output increase for the five individual sectors studied in this report.

The estimate was produced through the following steps. First, from the "uses" table, the percent of intermediary input use from other sectors of the economy per unit of value added generated in each of the five sectors was calculated. Since the Dead Sea mineral processing would be a new activity, it was assumed that the stone quarrying and processing industry would be a good proxy for the share of intermediary input use in total output so the same ratio was used. To avoid double counting, inputs used from the other four sectors were excluded from the total value of intermediary inputs used by the sector. Second, the ratios calculated in the first step were multiplied by the estimates of potential value added that could be generated in each of the five sectors. Third, these sums were added

Methodological Notes

to calculate the amount of output required from other sectors to generate the estimated amount of potential value added in the five sectors, which are the focus of this report. Fourth, data from the same Supply and Uses Tables were used to calculate the weighted average ratio of gross output to value added for all sectors of the Palestinian economy, which is equal to 0.54. Finally, the total value of the multiplier effect was calculated by multiplying the value obtained in the third step by 0.54.

The value of the multiplier estimated through the above steps is equal to 1.48 and this estimate is thought to be a relatively conservative one. Although this approach to estimating the multiplier ignores potential supply constraints, which might limit the supply response of some sectors to demand from one of the five sectors and lead to price increases (with negative effects on market-clearing quantities), the supply constraints are not too important in the medium and in particular the long run, when adequate time is given for supply to adjust. Therefore, they can be ignored. On the other hand, this approach ignores third round and subsequent round effects, as the production of intermediary inputs also requires the use of other intermediary inputs, thus underestimating the true spillover effect related to intersectoral linkages. However, the most important reason why the value of 1.48 represents a significant underestimation of the true multiplier is that the positive effects that could be attributed to the development of both physical and institutional infrastructure in Area C were not estimated in this report; yet, lifting the restrictions to allow infrastructure investments in Area C (in particular transportation infrastructure) would no doubt lead to a nonnegligible multiplier effect.

Sensitivity Analysis

As the above estimates show that the largest increases in value added could be expected as a result of investments in the Dead Sea mineral processing and agriculture increases, the overall estimate of potential value added is the most sensitive to changes in assumptions used to produce those two estimates. Consequently, if one were to assume that the potential value added that could be generated in the mineral processing industry would be equivalent to that in Jordan (rather than the average of Israel and Jordan), the estimate of potential value added that could be generated in this industry would drop by as much as 47 percent, or equivalently would increase by 47 percent if the potential was measured solely based on the value added in this industry in Israel. Second, if the quantity of potentially irrigable land is reduced by 30 percent from 394,000 dunum to 276,000 dunum, the estimate of value added in the agriculture sector would be reduced by 186 million, or 27 percent, given that it is estimated that 88 percent of the incremental value added would be generated on irrigated land, although it was assumed that the area of rain-fed land would be twice as large as that of irrigated land. On the other hand, although not very likely, increases in the quantity of potentially irrigable land in the West Bank would significantly increase the agriculture potential. The impact of more conservative assumptions in the remaining three sectors examined in this report would be substantially smaller. For instance, a 30 percent lower increase in mining and quarrying sector and the construction sector would reduce the estimated potential by about USD 70 million in each of the two sectors, respectively. Similar size effects on the estimated tourism output would be half as significant as the above two. As the estimate of the incremental output in the telecommunications sector is relatively small (USD 48 million), the total estimate of potential value added is least sensitive to more conservative assumptions in this sector. However, as noted in the report, Area C restrictions intertwined with other restrictions seriously threaten the viability of the Palestinian telecommunications industry as they prevent the introduction of 3G services. Given that this sector currently accounts for 6 percent of the Palestinian GDP, the downside potential of loosing market to Israeli competition could lead to a substantial negative impact on the Palestinian GDP.

Notes

1. PCBS, 2009a. "Agricultural Statistics 2007/2008."
2. MoNE and ARIJ, 2011, performed a similar exercise to compute the potential agricultural production value of the entire Palestinian territory.
3. The cropping area is equal to the actual cultivated area times the number of harvests in the year in that cultivated area. For instance, if a specific crop is harvested twice a year, then the cropping area for that crop would be double the actual cultivated land. Given the current cropping pattern, the cropping area in the Palestinian territory is estimated by the Palestinian Ministry of Agriculture to be 1.24 times larger than the actual cultivated area.
4. PCBS, 2009, records the effective land cultivated already incorporating the multiseasonal farming adjustment.

    The estimates of the cultivated land are based on the agricultural statistics for 2007/08 (PCBS, 2009a) rather than the agricultural census of 2010 (PCBS, 2011) as the latter severely underestimates the total cultivated land by focusing on a restrictive definition of agricultural holdings. The census classifies as such only the land which is at least 1 dunum of open cultivation or at least 0.5 dunum of protected cultivation. However a large number of land plots in the West Bank fall below these thresholds and are not considered. That appears to be the main reason why the census estimates the cultivated land in the West Bank to be 934,933 dunum against 1,693,742 dunum recorded in PCBS (2009). The latter figure is also close to the one recorded by LRC (2010).
5. The total irrigated effective cropping area in Gaza is 115,413 dunum (PCBS, 2009), which is considered to be equal to the potentially irrigable area (Glover and Hunter, 2010).
6. Palestinian Ministry of Agriculture (2012). Characteristics of Natural Rangelands in the West Bank, Ramallah.
7. PCBS, 2009a. "Agricultural Statistics 2007/2008."
8. A geological survey for Area C would have enabled the authors to make a more accurate estimate of potential stone deposits there. Unfortunately, no geological survey for Area C has been carried out.

Methodological Notes

9. This is probably a very conservative estimate for several reasons: first, because many of the existing quarries have been largely depleted, in particular the handful legally operating in Area C; second, because Area C is much less sparsely populated than Areas A and B; third, the estimates do not include a very substantial potential of aggregates production for both the Palestinian and Israeli markets.
10. In figure A.1, the value of output is given by the areas (p';q') in the case with the restrictions and (p";q") in the case without the restrictions.
11. This figure is based on market research conducted by the landline operator.
12. The national landline operator prefers not to publically disclose the figure for the monthly ARPU for landline and ADSL. The figure was, however, shared with the World Bank staff on confidential basis and was used to calculate the amount of potential revenues lost due to the inability to expand the company's customer base in Area C.
13. Of course, it would be unreasonable to argue that the removal of restrictions on tourism development in Area C would be a sufficient enabler for utilizing this whole economic potential, as the demand is affected by other factors, not least the real or perceived security risks, promotion and branding, and so on, and the building of tourism supply would require the removal of other restrictions on movement and access that affect not only private sector activity in West Bank and Gaza but also significant investments, knowhow, and so on. Nevertheless, the intrinsic comparative advantages that would enable the Palestinians to ultimately develop both the demand and supply to generate the amount of revenues, which is currently generated by Israel as a result of Dead Sea tourism, are in present on the Palestinian part of the Dead Sea shore.

APPENDIX B

Agriculture Section Tables

Table B.1 Value of Production Per Dunum and Cultivated Area, Irrigated vs. Rain-fed, Fruit Trees

	Irrigated		Rain fed	
	Area (dunum)	Value per dunum (USD)	Area (dunum)	Value per dunum (USD)
Olive	23,945	169	893,721	101
Grape	4,441	1,524	63,708	586
Valencia	9,684	2,399		
Lemon	4,874	4,700	405	1,369
Plum	246	572	21,155	355
Clement	2,368	1,285		
Fig	153	912	13,039	597
Shammoty	2,613	2,608		
Banana	1,280	3,059		
Guava	2,476	1,531		
Navel Oragne	1,795	2,007		
Aloe			4,894	698
Date	3,953	965	20	1,152
Almond (hard)	14	556	28,165	137
Almond (soft)	70	2,219	11,110	1,630
Poppy	951	1,598	0	
Grapefruit	—		529	904
Peach	535	818	2,053	307
Apricot	230	1,093	4,174	373
Apple	232	1,175	1,520	501
Cherry	30	845	1,708	1,170
Pomegranate	118	454	934	506
Mandarin	—		296	1,071
Akadenia	146	2,725	350	692
Mango	—		215	2,014
Avocado	—		84	3,762
Francawy	—		143	909
Walnut	—		293	1,727

table continues next page

Table B.1 Value of Production Per Dunum and Cultivated Area, Irrigated vs. Rain-fed, Fruit Trees *(continued)*

	Irrigated		Rain fed	
	Area (dunum)	Value per dunum (USD)	Area (dunum)	Value per dunum (USD)
Pears	44	580	411	454
Other citrus	—		71	1,662
Quince	28	1,039	251	669
Others	78	1,974	0	
Other stone fruit	140	843	0	
Custard	—		30	7,033
Bomaly	—		40	925
Sumak	—		424	752
Balady orange	—		20	1,800
Nectarine	10	664	44	417
Pican	24	2,788	26	2,734
Total	60,478	1,418	1,049,833	170

Source: PCBS (2009).

Table B.2 Value of Production per Dunum and Cultivated Area, Irrigated vs. Rain-fed, Field Crops

	Irrigated		Rain fed	
	Area (dunum)	Value per dunum (USD)	Area (dunum)	Value per dunum (USD)
Wheat	3,200	222	226,241	101
Barley	990	99	106,558	29
Sern	109	33	27,379	272
Clover	1,227	332	21,374	174
Potato	20,061	1,346	1,116	786
Dry onion	5,653	1,679	11,673	731
Vetch			16,190	33
Chickpeas			14,575	111
Lentil			11,395	44
Tobacco			4,372	611
Broad bean			3,994	71
Sesame			3,781	177
Thyme	1,601	2,566	610	292
Anise			2,137	365
Sweet potato	1,780	2,258		
Dry garlic	430	4,132	1,143	984
Other clover, sern			1,386	74
Broom corn			1,034	8
Black cumin			948	135
Onion tuber	735	1,096	187	450
Local tobacco			787	1,220
Sorghum	5	1,049	775	13

table continues next page

Table B.2 Value of Production per Dunum and Cultivated Area, Irrigated vs. Rain-fed, Field Crops *(continued)*

	Irrigated		Rain fed	
	Area (dunum)	Value per dunum (USD)	Area (dunum)	Value per dunum (USD)
Fenugreek	2	90	396	141
Safflower			323	136
Cumin			210	395
Dry cowpea	60	1,330	147	42
Meramieh	95	4,122	77	1,602
Other dry leumes	30	625	104	156
Ment	114	1,690	10	1,538
Others			122	180
Chamomile	83	855		
Sunflower			71	70
Tomak			50	220
Fiber	30	1,367		
Total	36,205	1,360	459,165	123

Source: PCBS (2009).

Table B.3 Value of Production Per Dunum and Cultivated Area, Irrigated vs. Rain-fed, Vegetables

	Irrigated		Rain fed	
	Area (dunum)	Value per dunum (USD)	Area (dunum)	Value per dunum (USD)
Cucumber	32,348	4,290		
Squash	22,263	1,488	5,922	440
Tomato	20,143	6,767	4,778	346
Eggplant	11,712	3,107	1	366
Maize	9,462	505		
Cauliflower	7,784	2,221	904	807
White cabbages	6,352	2,024	4	115
Snake cucumber	631	992	5,540	273
Okra	1,474	757	4,196	509
Jew's mallow	5,396	1,157		
Broad bean (green)	2,869	893	2,199	583
Hot pepper	4,527	3,002		
Kidney bean (green)	4,260	1,854	59	284
Peas	1,288	436	2,943	400
Chickpeas (green)	50	307	3,859	515
Watermelon	3,080	760	460	105
Paprika	2,796	312		
Spinach	1,885	1,672	509	1,035
Onion	1,355	1,636	845	687
Pumpkin	905	876	589	406
Parsley	1,378	1,536	34	333

table continues next page

Table B.3 Value of Production Per Dunum and Cultivated Area, Irrigated vs. Rain-fed, Vegetables *(continued)*

	Irrigated		Rain fed	
	Area (dunum)	Value per dunum (USD)	Area (dunum)	Value per dunum (USD)
Carrot	1,373	1,076		
Cowpea	579	1,404	766	268
Strawberry	1,260	3,453		
Muskmelon	903	1,103	300	455
Radish	1,052	1,352	84	200
Turnip	864	2,621	54	249
Lettuce	882	1,112	36	87
Fennen	701	4,044		
Gourd	245	1,454	372	327
Kidney bean (yellow)	448	1,750		
Chard	429	1,793		
Cut flower	406	8,239		
Others	337	8,080		
Red cabbages	182	1,401		
Warak lesan	77	1,545		
Garlic (green)	8	3,778	5	756
Taro	12	2,917		
Total	**151,716**	**2,947**	**34,459**	**435**

Source: PCBS (2009).

APPENDIX C

Relevant Legal Agreements

Oslo Agreement, Annex III, Protocol on Israeli-Palestinian Cooperation in Economic and Development Programs

The two sides agree to establish an Israeli-Palestinian continuing Committee for Economic Cooperation, focusing, among other things, on the following:

1. Cooperation in the field of water, including a Water Development Program prepared by experts from both sides, which will also specify the mode of cooperation in the management of water resources in the Palestinian territories, and will include proposals for studies and plans on water rights of each party, as well as on the equitable utilization of joint water resources for implementation in and beyond the interim period.
2. Cooperation in the field of electricity, including an Electricity Development Program, which will also specify the mode of cooperation for the production, maintenance, purchase and sale of electricity resources.
3. Cooperation in the field of energy, including an Energy Development Program, which will provide for the exploitation of oil and gas for industrial purposes, particularly in the Gaza Strip and in the Negev, and will encourage further joint exploitation of other energy resources. This Program may also provide for the construction of a Petrochemical industrial complex in the Gaza Strip and the construction of oil and gas pipelines.
4. Cooperation in the field of finance, including a Financial Development and Action Program for the encouragement of international investment in the West Bank and the Gaza Strip, and in Israel, as well as the establishment of a Palestinian Development Bank.
5. Cooperation in the field of transport and communications, including a Program, which will define guidelines for the establishment of a Gaza Sea Port Area, and will provide for the establishing of transport and communications lines to and from the West Bank and the Gaza Strip to Israel and to other countries. In addition, this Program will provide for carrying out the necessary construction of roads, railways, communications lines, etc.

6. Cooperation in the field of trade, including studies, and Trade Promotion Programs, which will encourage local, regional and inter-regional trade, as well as a feasibility study of creating free trade zones in the Gaza Strip and in Israel, mutual access to these zones, and cooperation in other areas related to trade and commerce.
7. Cooperation in the field of industry, including Industrial Development Programs, which will provide for the establishment of joint Israeli-Palestinian Industrial Research and Development Centers, will promote Palestinian-Israeli joint ventures, and provide guidelines for cooperation in the textile, food, pharmaceutical, electronics, diamonds, computer and science-based industries.
8. A program for cooperation in, and regulation of, labor relations and cooperation in social welfare issues.
9. A Human Resources Development and Cooperation Plan, providing for joint Israeli-Palestinian workshops and seminars, and for the establishment of joint vocational training centers, research institutes and data banks.
10. An Environmental Protection Plan, providing for joint and/or coordinated measures in this sphere.
11. A program for developing coordination and cooperation in the field of communication and media.
12. Any other programs of mutual interest.

The Israeli-Palestinian Interim Agreement on the West Bank and the Gaza Strip ("Oslo 2"— 9/28/95)—ANNEX III, ARTICLE 36, Telecommunications

A. General

1. This sphere includes, inter alia, the management and monitoring of the use of the radio frequency spectrum, the use of the geostationary satellite orbit, the planning, formulation and implementation of telecommunications policies, regulations and legal frameworks. The above shall be in accordance with, and subject to, the following provisions:
2.
    a. In Area C, although powers and responsibilities are transferred to the Palestinian side, any digging or building regarding telecommunications and any installation of telecommunication equipment, will be subject to prior confirmation of the Israeli side, through the Civil Affairs Coordination and Cooperation Committee CAC.
    b. Notwithstanding paragraph a. above, the supply of telecommunications services in Area C to the Settlements and military locations, and the activities regarding the supply of such services, shall be under the powers and responsibilities of the Israeli side.

B. Principles

1. Israel recognizes that the Palestinian side has the right to build and operate separate and independent communication systems and infrastructures including telecommunication networks, a television network and a radio network.

2. Without prejudice to subparagraph D.5.c of this section, the Palestinian side has the right to establish satellite networks for various services, excluding international services.
3. The Palestinian side has the right to establish its own telecommunications policies, systems and infrastructures. The Palestinian side also has the right to choose any and all kinds of communication systems (including broadcasting systems) and technologies, suitable for its future in, inter alia, basic and value added services (including cellular telephony).
4. Operators and providers of services, presently and in the future, in the West Bank and the Gaza Strip shall be required to obtain the necessary approvals from the Palestinian side. In addition, all those operating and/or providing services, presently and in the future, in the West Bank and the Gaza Strip who wish to operate and/or provide services in Israel, are required to obtain the necessary approvals from the Israeli Ministry of Communications.
5. Both sides shall refrain from any action that interferes with the communication and broadcasting systems and infrastructures of the other side. Specifically, the Palestinian side shall ensure that only those frequencies and channels specified in Schedule 5: List of Approved Frequencies (herein—"Schedule 5") and Schedule 6: List of Approved TV Channels and the Location of Transmitters (herein—"Schedule 6") shall be used and that it shall not disturb or interfere with Israeli radio communication activity, and Israel shall ensure that there shall be no disturbance of or interference with the said frequencies and channels.
6. A joint committee of technical experts representing both sides shall be established to address any issue arising out of this section including the growing future needs of the Palestinian side (hereinafter referred to as "the Joint Technical Committee" or "JTC"). The JTC shall meet on a regular basis for the purpose of solving all relevant problems, and as necessary in order to solve urgent problems.

C. *The Electromagnetic Sphere*

1. The Palestinian side has the right to use the radio frequency spectrum, in accordance with principles acceptable to both sides, for present and future needs, and frequencies assigned or reassigned within the West Bank and the Gaza Strip covering all its required services within the bands L.F., M.F., H.F., V.H.F., U.H.F., S.H.F. and E.H.F. In order to satisfy the present needs of the Palestinian side, the frequencies detailed in Schedule 5 are assigned for the use of the Palestinian side in the West Bank and the Gaza Strip.
2. Future needs for frequencies shall be agreed upon by the two sides. To that end, the Palestinian side shall present its requirements through the JTC which must fulfill these requirements within a period not exceeding one month. Frequencies or sections of frequencies shall be assigned, or an alternative thereto providing the required service within the same band, or the best alternative thereto acceptable by the Palestinian side, and agreed upon by Israel in the JTC.

3.
   a. The frequencies specified in Schedule 5 shall serve, inter alia, for the transmission of a television network and a radio network.
   b. The television channels and locations of transmitters to be used by the Palestinian side are specified in Schedule 6. The production studios and related broadcasting equipment shall be located in the West Bank and the Gaza Strip.
   c. The radio transmitter shall be located in the area of Ramallah and Al-Bireh Cities, at the presently agreed site.
   d. The Palestinian side has the right to change the location(s) of radio transmitters according to an agreement between the two sides through the JTC, to serve the Palestinian plans in achieving the best coverage.

D. Telecommunications

1. Pending the establishment of an independent Palestinian telephone network, the Palestinian side shall enter into a commercial agreement with Bezeq—The Israel Telecommunications Corp. Ltd. (herein, "Bezeq"), regarding supply of certain services in the West Bank and the Gaza Strip. In the area of international telephony, commercial agreement(s) shall be concluded with Bezeq or other duly-licensed Israeli companies. The above shall be without prejudice to subparagraph 5.c below.
2. As long as the Palestinian network is integrated with the Israeli network, the Palestinian side shall use such telephonic equipment as is compatible with the standards adopted and applied in Israel by the Ministry of Communications, and will coordinate with the Israeli side any changes to the structure and form of telephone exchanges and transmission equipment. The Palestinian side shall be permitted to import and use any and all kinds of telephones, fax machines, answering machines, modems, and data terminals, without having to comply with the above-mentioned standards (accordingly, lists A1 and A2 of Annex V (Protocol on Economic Relations) will be updated). Israel recognizes and understands that for the purpose of building a separate network, the Palestinian side has the right to adopt its own standards and to import equipment which meets these standards (accordingly, lists A1 and A2 of Annex V (Protocol on Economic Relations) will be updated). The equipment will be used only when the independent Palestinian network is operational.
3.
   a. The Palestinian side shall enable the supply of telecommunications services to the Settlements and the military installations by Bezeq, as well as the maintenance by Bezeq of the telecommunications infrastructure serving them and the infrastructure crossing the areas under the territorial jurisdiction of the Palestinian side.
   b. The Israeli side shall enable the supply of telecommunications services to the geographically-dispersed areas within the West Bank and the Gaza Strip. This shall include provision, subject to the approval of the proper Israeli authorities, free of charge, of rights of way or sites in the West Bank

for microwave repeater stations and cables to interlink the West Bank and to connect the West Bank with the Gaza Strip.
   c. Israel recognizes the right of the Palestinian side to establish telecommunications links (microwave and physical) to connect the West Bank and the Gaza Strip through Israel. The modalities of establishing such telecommunications connections, and their maintenance, shall be agreed upon by the two sides. The protection of the said connections shall be under the responsibility of Israel.
4. Without prejudice to paragraph 3 above:
   a. The Palestinian side shall take the necessary measures to ensure the protection of the telecommunication infrastructures serving Israel, the Settlements and the military installations, which are located in the areas under the territorial jurisdiction of the Palestinian side.
   b. The Israeli side shall take the necessary measures to ensure the protection of the telecommunication infrastructures serving the West Bank and the Gaza Strip and which are located in areas under Israel's responsibility.
5.
   a. The Palestinian side has the right to collect revenue for all internal and international telecommunication services originating and terminating in the West Bank and the Gaza Strip (except Settlements and military locations).
   b. Details regarding payment by the Palestinian side to Bezeq or other duly-licensed Israeli companies, and compensation by Bezeq or the said companies to the Palestinian side, referred to in subparagraph a. above, shall be agreed upon in the commercial agreement(s) between them.
   c. The provisions of subparagraphs a. and b. above will be applied between the sides until such time as the two sides agree upon installation and operation of an "international gateway", as well as the international code, for the Palestinian side and the actual commencement of operation of the said gateway.
   d. The Palestinian side shall enter into a discussion with Bezeq for the purpose of coming to an agreement for the use of a separate area code and numbering plan, pending the establishment of a separate Palestinian network.
6. The Palestinian side has the right to collect taxes on all telecommunications services billed in the West Bank and the Gaza Strip, subject to the provisions of Annex V (Protocol on Economic Relations).
   a. The Israeli side shall provide the Palestinian side with all operating, maintenance and system manuals, information regarding billing systems and all operating and computer programming protocols of all the equipment that will be transferred to the Palestinian side, subject to protection of rights of commercial confidentiality.
   b. The Israeli side shall also supply the Palestinian side with all contractual agreements between the Civil Administration and all domestic and international entities in the area of telecommunications. The timing of the

provision of the above mentioned materials will be as provided for in this Annex.

c. Bezeq, in accordance with the commercial agreement, will supply the Palestinian side with all legal verification of its purported ownership of any and all movable or immovable assets in the West Bank and the Gaza Strip, that are not part of the Civil Administration's present network.

Bibliography

ARIJ database. 2012 & 2013

Atyani, A., and B. Makhool. 2004. "Cost Structure, Economies of Scale, and Their Effect on the Competetiveness of Palestinian Industries." Palestine Economic Policy Research Institute (MAS), Gaza and West Bank.

Berdegue, J. A., E. Ramirez, T. Reardon, and G. Escobar. 2001. "Rural Nonfarm Employment and Incomes in Chile." *World Development* 29 (3): 411–25.

Bimkom. 2008. "The Prohibited Zone: Israeli Planning Policy in the Palestinian Villages in Area C." June.

B'tselem. 2011. "Dispossession and Exploitation. Israel's Policy in the Jordan Valley and the Northern Dead Sea." Epalestine.com.

———. 2010a. "The Separation Barrier." http://www.btselem.org.

———. 2010b. "By Hook and by Crook: Israeli Settlement Policy in the West Bank." July.

———. 2011. "Taking Control of Land." http://www.btselem.org/

Cali, M., and S. Miaari. 2013. "The Labor Market Impact of Mobility Restrictions: Evidence from the West Bank." Policy Research Working Paper 6457, World Bank, Poverty Reduction and Economic Management Network, International Trade Department, Washington, DC.

CNN Money. 2009. "Turning Dead Sea Mud into Honey." http://www.israeltrade.org.au/spotlight-on-israels-cosmetics-industry/.

Cosmetics & Toiletries. " Organic Personal Care Products, Market for Skin Care, Hair Care, Oral Care and Cosmetics—Global Industry Analysis, Size, Share, Growth, Trends and Forecast, 2012–2018." http://www.cosmeticsandtoiletries.com/formulating/category/natural/Demand-for-Organic-Beauty-to-Grow-to-Over-13-Billion-by-2018-Report-Says-213160491.html.

De Jonge, J., 2012. "Palestinian Land Development Needs Assessment (2012)." Report commissioned by a Consortium of European Palestinian Land Development Program Donors, Ramallah.

Dudeen, B. A., 2002. "Land Degradation in Palestine: Main Factors, Present Status and Trends." Land Research Center, Hebron.

Estache, A., B. Speciale, and D. Veredas. 2005. "How Much Does Infrastructure Matter to Growth in Sub-Saharan Africa." European Center for Advanced Research in Economics Working Paper, Universite Libre de Bruxelles, Belgium.

Gisha—Legal Center for Freedom of Movement. 2012. "What is 'The Separation Policy'?" June.

Glover, S., and A. Hunter. 2010. "Meeting Future Palestinian Water Needs." Economic Policy Research Institute (MAS), Jerusalem.

Haaretz. 2012. March 30. http://www.haaretz.com/news/diplomacy-defense/israel-defense-ministry-plan-earmarks-10-percent-of-west-bank-for-settlement-expansion-1.421589.

Horváth, Endre, and Douglas C. Frechtling. 1999. "Estimating the Multiplier Effects of Tourism Expenditures on a Local Economy through a Regional Input-Output Model."*Journal of Travel Research* 37 (May): 324–32.

ICL. 2012. "Periodic Report." Israel.

IMF. 2012. "West Bank and Gaza: Labor Market Trends, Growth and Unemployment." IMF.

IPCC. 2013. "Action Plan: Planning Intervention in Area C." mimeo.

Israeli Central Bureau of Statistics. Input-Output tables 2006.

———. Time Series DataBank.

Israeli Nature and Parks Authority. 2012. "Annual Report." Tel Aviv University.

Israeli-Palestinian Interim Agreement on the West Bank and Gaza Strip.

Jordanian Ministry of Tourism and Antiquities' Tourism Statistical Newsletter.

Land Research Center. 2010. "Land Suitability for Reclamation April 2010 and Development in the West Bank." Hebron.

Lanjouw, P., and A. Shariff. 2002. "Rural Nonfarm Employment in India: Access, Income, and Poverty Impact." Working Paper Series no 81, National Council of Applied Economic Research, New Delhi.

Malpezzi, S., and S. K. Mayo. 1987. "The Demand for Housing in Developing Countries: Empirical Estimates from Household Data." *Economic Development and Cultural Change* 35 (4): 687–721.

Ministry of Finance of Palestinian Authority Fiscal Data, 2012.

MoNE and Arij. 2011. "The Economic Costs of the Israeli Occupation for the Occupied Palestinian Terriroty."

Munayyer, Y. 2012. *When Settlers Attack*. Washington DC: The Palestine Center.

Navot. 2013. "Israeli Settler Agriculture: As a Means of Land Takeover in the West Bank."

OCHA. 2009. "Restricting Space: The Planning Regime Applied by Israel in Area c of the West Bank." East Jerusalem, December 15.

Palestinian Ministry of Agriculture. 2012. "Characteristics of Natural Rangelands in the West Bank." Ramallah.

Palestinian Water Authority. 2012. "National Water Strategy for Palestine." Ramallah.

PCBS. "Hotel Activities in Palestine: Annual Bulletin" (Various years)." Ramallah, Palestine.

———. "Labor Force Survey" (Various years). Ramallah, Palestine.

———. "Survey of the Perceptions of Owners/Managers of Active Industrial Enterprises Regarding the Economic Situation, Q1 2013." Ramallah, Palestine.

———. "Tourism Activities Survey" (Various years). Ramallah, Palestine.

PCBS. 2004. "Supply and Uses Tables." Preliminary results. Ramallah, Palestine.

PCBS. 2008. "Population Census, 2007." Ramallah, Palestine.

———. 2011. "Agricultural Census 2010." Ramallah, Palestine.

———. 2009a. "Agricultural Statistics 2007/2008." Ramallah, Palestine.

———. 2009b. "Housing Projections up to 2017." Ramallah, Palestine.

———. 2009c. "Water Statistics in the Palestinian Territory Annual Report, 2008." Ramallah, Palestine.

———. 2010. "Industry Statistics." Ramallah, Palestine.

———. 2011. "A Special Bulletin on the Palestinians." Ramallah, Palestine.

———. 2012a. "Palestinian National Accounts 2011." Ramallah, Palestine.

———. 2012b. "Palestinian Labor Force Survey 2011." Ramallah, Palestine.

———. 2012c. "Palestinian National Accounts 2011." Ramallah, Palestine.

———. 2012d. "Palestinian National Accounts 2011." Ramallah, Palestine

Selby, Jan. 2013. "Cooperation, Domination and Colonization: The Israeli-Palestinian Joint Water Committee." *Water Alternatives* 6 (1): 1–24.

Taipei Times. "Jordan Eying a Big Share of Dead Sea Cosmetics Market." http://www.taipeitimes.com/News/bizfocus/archives/2010/03/21/2003468511.

Union of Stone and Marble Industry. 2011. "Stone & Marble Industry in Palestine: Developing a Strategy for the Future." http://blair.3cdn.net/328bd530dca6a02f4c_kum6b6dhi.pdf.

UN OCHA. 2009. "Restricting Space: The Planning Regime Applied by Israel in Area C of the West Bank."

———. 2012. "West Bank Movement and Access Update." East Jerusalem.

US Geological Survey. 2011. "Minerals Yearbook."

Who Profits. 2012. "Made in Israel: Agricultural Export from Occupied Territories." Tel Aviv, Israel.

World Bank. 2007. "Movement and Access Restrictions in the West Bank: Uncertainty and Inefficiency in the Palestinian Economy." May.

———. 2008a. "Palestinian Economic Prospects: Aid, Access, and Reform, Economic Monitoring Report to the Ad Hoc Liaison Committee." September.

———. 2008b. "The Economic Effects of Restricted Access to Land in the West Bank."

———. 2009. "Assessment of Restrictions on Palestinian Water Sector Development." Sector Note.

———. 2010. "The Underpinnings of the Future Palestinian State: Sustainable Growth and Institutions."

Yesh Din. 2009. "Petition for an Order Nisi and an Interim Injunction." The Supreme Court of Israel, Jerusalem.

Environmental Benefits Statement

The World Bank is committed to reducing its environmental footprint. In support of this commitment, the Publishing and Knowledge Division leverages electronic publishing options and print-on-demand technology, which is located in regional hubs worldwide. Together, these initiatives enable print runs to be lowered and shipping distances decreased, resulting in reduced paper consumption, chemical use, greenhouse gas emissions, and waste.

The Publishing and Knowledge Division follows the recommended standards for paper use set by the Green Press Initiative. Whenever possible, books are printed on 50 percent to 100 percent postconsumer recycled paper, and at least 50 percent of the fiber in our book paper is either unbleached or bleached using Totally Chlorine Free (TCF), Processed Chlorine Free (PCF), or Enhanced Elemental Chlorine Free (EECF) processes.

More information about the Bank's environmental philosophy can be found at http://crinfo.worldbank.org/wbcrinfo/node/4.

www.ingramcontent.com/pod-product-compliance
Lightning Source LLC
Chambersburg PA
CBHW081258170426
43198CB00017B/2838